"THE FROG BLOG, LEARNING ON A LILY PAD"

By Christina M. Eder

**Cover design illustrated by Joseph "Red Paint" Spillman

EVOLUTION OF "THE FROG BLOG, LEARNING ON A LILY PAD"

I began writing the FROG blog in 2017 to share my Fully Relying On God experiences. The original musings evolved into a series of less-than-500 word essays about seeing God in everyday occurrences.

Currently, sci-fi, fantasy, and romance are the top-selling book genres. I'll categorize this book as romance because I'm learning and practicing to love God in the most unconditional way I know. I want our relationship to be exclusive. I've dated Him for many years and now find myself thinking of Him more often and seeing Him more frequently. He desires my full commitment. I appreciate His power, His truth, and His unlimited resources so in this romance collection, I share details about some of the ways He spoils me rotten, and loves the spoiled rotten out of me.

One of my original plans for this FROG project was to publish a collection of 100 short love stories. In August 2018, I finished writing 103 love letters to God and asked my editor to vote three of the letters off the island, or lily pad, as the case may be in a FROG blog.

Fast forward. While waiting for my book *Life's Too Short for Dull Razors, Cheap Pens, and Worn-Out Underwear* to be published, I worked out a budget for the *FROG Blog, Love Letters from a Lily Pad*. God gently swirled the waters of my mind and offered a new wave of thought for this creation. Instead of 100 blogs, I was to publish only 77 essays.

My response to His new direction for my project?

"What? But Lord! I have written, edited, rewritten, reedited 77 plus 26! I'm already cutting back 3 of my essays because 100 will be a nice round number. Besides, I don't want to waste any of these reflections because each letter is a chance to show that You are my Main Man in this romantic collection of stories!"

The seemingly odd number didn't make sense to me. This book was on its way to the editor's desk. I had the dirty green paper budgeted. Concerned that last minute publishing jitters were drowning out my logic, I questioned God about my understanding the direction His book was taking. (This wasn't the first 1000th time I've approached God with my doubt).

A few weeks after that clarification plea, the reasoning behind the number 77 became clearer. Biblically, seven represents completion and unity. Seventy-seven completed my part of this unity. *"Ahhhhhhhhh. Wisely clever Lord. Got it. So let's get started right away! What am I to do with the 26 remaining essays I wrote? Should I use them toward another book? And if there's another book, does that mean it'll be another FROG blog collection or something else?"*

I think God sent an eye roll with a gentle exhale as if to say, "Christina, you write from the Martha and Mary Studio. Let's not let Martha overpower Mary on this mission? One leap at a time please."

That began a spirited conversational tennis match with God in September 2018:

Christina: Which of the 77 essays should I resubmit to my editor?

God: There are 23 other artists who have stories to share about FROG moments."

Christina: "OK!" Those 23 will fill the gap between 77 and 100. That means I can still publish 100 reflections as I had planned!

God: "I will show you who they are and they will illustrate their FROG experience according to My leading."

Christina: "Great, I know of a lot of writers with incredible stories.

God: "The artists aren't all writers."

Christina: "Lord, I know not everyone is a natural writer, but we can work out the edits later."

God: "I said I'd lead you to 23 other artists. Artists aren't only writers."

Christina: "Oh!"

God: "Some artists will tell their FROG experience through photos, poems, drawings, writing, or songs."

Christina: "Ok, got it. So when you give me the list of artists, I'll contact them and ask for their FROG experience using the craft that they choose?"

God: "Not yet."

Christina: "How about November 25th as the artist's deadline? That was my Mom's earthly birthday and it'd be meaningful to use November 25th as a benchmark for this project. It's the end of September so I'd have almost two months to organize and align this with her birthday. FROG experiences are a celebration of life and it'd be neat to use this book to honor Mom."

God: "Trust me. I'll work out details."

Fast forward through October. From the Martha and Mary Writing Studio, 'Martha' grew uptight. God hadn't given me further instructions and I didn't receive any direction about how to weave 23 yet-to-be-revealed artists into this book. I finally called Beth Erickson, my high school friend, who once encouraged (i.e. strongly suggested) me to write a column for our school newspaper, *Quibbles and Bits*.

She is a professional writer and editor and I knew she'd give me honest wisdom. Beth is also a main root beneath helping me grow writing as a childhood hobby into what became my career. *The Quibbles and Bits* column had a similar tone as *The FROG Blog*.

I awkwardly explained this project to her, uncertain about how to proceed, unsure if there was even a market for what I crafted. Partway through our phone conversation I asked her to be the first of my twenty-three artists to share her FROG experience. Her "yes" opened another new door for me to create this collection.

Shortly after Beth agreed to write her FROG reflection, God gave me a few names to contact, including a husband/wife music ministry team, a photographer, and a monologue writer. The calendar was closing in on November 25th and I wanted submissions to meet my Mom's birth date. I had 8 of the 23 names. I knew God guided me to include other people. I thought my next step was to fish the artist pool for the remaining 15 of the 23 people. (Just in case God needed back-up ideas for artists, I offered 4 additional contacts waiting in the wings if some artists declined this project invitation. Ahem).

The 8 artists, from God's guidance, had accepted the anthology invitation, even though a few were hesitant about their abilities. I contacted some of the remaining 15 artists from my list, but received no response. I now realize I was using a FROM (Fully Rely On Me) method to force the book's birth. I had tried building this project with "my" people first and then hoped, assumed, figured God would jump on my scaffolding to finish "my" construction.

When I finally repelled from my virtual skyscraper, to an altitude where my own hot air is less dense, God excavated the next beam. He clarified that 22 of the 23 artists would be from the Oak Ridge, TN area where I originally met these people with FROG experiences. I was learning to trust His timing, His idea, His reason. Still learning!

Through this intense process that exposed much of my weakness, I've gotten a glimpse at maybe what God anticipates when we all meet in heaven. In reading these vulnerable reflections, I often found myself unable to sleep at night or sit still. I wanted to have unlimited hours to meet each artist one-on-one to digest every line, memory, or picture that birthed their story.

If my craving to hear details from 23 snapshots of 23 people's lives has grown so strong, I *need* eternity to listen to the rest of their life experience! It flabbergasts me to picture heaven including billions and billions of other FROG-ers. Thank God we won't require sleep or be limited by stopwatch lifestyles.

I headline this anthology with 77 FROG Blogs. The Encore of 23 follows my opening act. This is a collection of trusting artists who share transparency about how we Fully Relied On God. I (now) treasure a tedious development of my first anthology. I read, cried, laughed, prayed, and concocted facial expressions that could possibly end up as a new Emoji characters. I'm humbled, honored, and excited to share God's work through our hearts.

Loving deeper from the lily pad, Christina

JUMPING FROM A LILY PAD INTO AN OCEAN

I am energized from the craft of writing. It's a spiritual boost of caffeine and lately I haven't regularly steeped in that literary jolt. As a result, some of my joy has been depleted. As I was tracing the source of this dark funk, I discovered a sharp lightning bolt of revelation. I stopped writing as often because I haven't created an outlet for its finished product. I journal large segments to express myself but those entries are not for public consumption. I have several orphaned pieces waiting for a home, eager to be placed on the "waiting to be adopted" list. Those words have full hearts, great spirit, and a tremendous need to be heard. However, I've kept that collection of sentences, paragraphs, and pages locked inside the safe walls of my journal. I feared that my waif words would be rejected by audiences that may judge my viewpoint or assume they understand what is inside of me.

I recently began participating in the 52 Virtues Project to develop the best version of myself. http://www.52virtues.com/virtues/the-virtues-project.php This week's featured virtue is courage. As a leap of courage, I am birthing The FROG BLOG. FROG is an acronym for Fully Rely On God. With courage, I'm making myself vulnerable (and stronger) by placing my words on the adoption table, the reading auction block. As the "mother" of these heartstrings, whether I'm the only one who reads about each birth blog or a particular blog goes viral, I will FROG my way.

With courage, Christina

THE PINK SLIP

Tomorrow I begin a new career assignment! I am honored, excited, filled (more like overflowing) with joy. As part of this gratefulness, I'm issuing my own career pink slip. This isn't a cynical foreshadowing that I'm going to be written up or reprimanded. This pink slip is written with a list of all the reasons and leadings toward why I'm taking this position. While I know this role is divinely appointed, in my humanness, there will be a day, or several days, when tasks show up as anything *but* divine.

Because I am leaving a nearly two year career of restaurant work, my appreciative pink slip includes a work week that coincides with my husband's job hours. It applauds a steady income. It embraces freedom from Friday nights and serving the stereotypical weekend crowd. The list gushes with breathtaking beauty of the farm-like surroundings, the small school atmosphere established on values deeply woven into my DNA. There are certain people who are named in this pink slip who will mentor me. There are future friendships to be crafted into this section of my life tapestry.

The "warning notice" to my spirit is literally written on pink paper (with a pink envelope to further seal the deal). I have requested our principal to add it to my personnel file as fire insurance, as a dashboard light indicator. When my flame threatens to be extinguished, this pink slip will fan the fire. When flesh fatigue and career battle wounds show up on my GPS (Gigantic Personal Selfishness), this pink slip will testify as my dashboard warning light. It will serve as a reminder to regularly maintain and service this vehicle of opportunity with new tread and fresh oil.

To bright pink beginnings among the life giving green lily pads of life, Christina

QUOTA

Much calculation from the FROG blog. For someone who defaults to words over numbers, today I projected figures with the vigor of an accountant.

My current book is at the publisher's house and I'm in the *Martha and Mary Studio* writing another book. I had residual inertia after meeting recent deadlines, which I prefer calling resurrection lines. Resurrection lines invite me to reference life over death. I was piddling through the pond, paddling for direction toward the upcoming endeavor. My waves of activity were more like a dog paddle. I was treading water and the only headway came from swimming thoughts.

To stop tangling my efforts in seaweed, I set guidelines. I committed to write ten pages each day. Anticipated writing time or energy bonuses would allow me to meet a sixty-page weekly quota. I was on fire! I let my increasing pace of outlined accomplishments swell and when I reached the end of my water trail, this project was written, edited, and published by month end! Feeling accomplished for planning to plan my plan, I looked at the page I started prior to my figurative whirlpool. Two sentences. Nine pages and forty-eight lines shy of my daily goal, but the day was not over.

What if Jesus set rigid daily, weekly, and monthly goals like I do? While He was on earth, what if He began each day on a numbers mission? Did His prayers resemble mine? Imagine Jesus in His quiet time: "God, it's Me, Your only Son. I know You want every knee to bow and everybody to believe in You. To complete Your will, today I'll heal nine lepers and part one large body of water. By next week I'll raise two people from the dead and feed 10,000 people. By month end, I'll seize a storm and walk on water. Oh! And God? To clarify? The water I walk on at month-end will be different than the body of water I originally parted. That was so last month. Before I jump into My robe and grab My sandals today, do You have any closing remarks?"

Back to my writing studio. If I meet each standard every day, do I advance to some unforeseen level of accomplishment? When I pursue every page line to chase a ghost of some mysterious quota, do I become a published phantom master? Or do I query the Author for His copyright and trademark seal of approval? It's *His* stories written *through* me.

"Lord, help me get Your go ahead before I go ahead. Guide me to balance my books with Your Book. Align my projects with Your projections. Guard me against excessive benchmarks merely for the sake of more bookmarks. Sift my writing through Your filter. I want every chapter of every day to read like a love story between You and me."

Checking in from His Publishing Clearinghouse, Christina

LESS IS MORE

Less is more, even less is even more. This is a guideline an English professor taught about writing and editing. He talked me about cutting excessive words (i.e that, just, then, definitely) to tighten story lines. A journalism teacher taught to write like an inverted pyramid in order of most-to-least important points. Tig, my husband, uses these journalism tools when speaking. My sister affectionately calls him *The One Word Wonder Man* because when Tig listens to our nonstop dialogue, he responds to a winded conversation with one word. Some of his classic one-word wonder hits include 'harsh', 'impressive', 'wild', and 'awesome'.

Jesus also teaches from the less is more approach. I opened a "red letter version" of the Bible and even though most scripture is written in black, the words Jesus communicates are penned in red. Based on the black-to-red word ratio, Jesus is frugal with what He speaks. Limited "red words," shows Jesus is not a babbler. He wisely chooses His word count to instruct. He used five loaves and two fish to feed 10,000 people. He guides us toward priority living when He teaches, "…Truly I tell you, whatever you did for one of the least of these brothers and sisters of mine, you did for me" (Mt. 25:40 NIV). Jesus speaks through His actions.

My intent for these essays is to use the "least of these" theme, to gather my ponderings from the FROG blog into one-page reflections. This "500 words or less" idea birthed from a study about increased fragmented reading and listening. Instead of my original discouragement about people missing the value of longer, more complete thoughts, I will go with the flow of this current stream of thinking. If Jesus can do a lot with a little and Tig can summarize my dissertations with one word, I'll graciously follow suit.

In 500 words or less, Christina

A PAT Answer

I am drawn to acronyms. I appreciate businesses using acronyms to creatively advertise ways to remember their business. In school, I retained data best when teachers attached an acronym to help students recall facts. There has been an increase of acronyms and sometimes the same base name is attached with different words for each letter.

For example, DOT refers to the Department of Transportation and the Description of Occupational Titles. One DOT will lead toward a vehicle related path, the other DOT will connect to a listing of every job from clowning to CFO (Chief Financial Officer or perhaps Chief Fire Officer).

I have not retained every acronym in my 50 revolutions around the sun, but EGBDF and ROYGBIV are burned in my memory. Every Good Boy Does Fine (EGBDF) jogged my memory for treble clef lines when I played piano. ROYGBIV provided a colorful way to remember a rainbow's order of colors to be Red, Orange, Yellow, Green, Blue, Indigo, and Violet. If there was no "I" in ROYGBIV, I would not have discovered that indigo was the color between blue and violet.

To collect another acronym for my mental files, I add a PAT answer. I have significant decisions on the table of the lily pad. These decisions present "opportunities for me to practice temperance. " Translate: personal invitations toward anxious thoughts. While I arrange and rearrange options, I initially wish I had only one solution instead of decision-making overload. I gain resolution in pat answer form. Pray And Trust (PAT).

Ironically, someone who is aware of my pending decisions advised me to simply trust the process. Her name? Of course! Pat. When Miss Pat first imparted her wisdom, I frequently used her mantra to trust the process. Trusting the process is simple to hear, an easy phrase to understand, and a tougher virtue to practice. Without choices, I wouldn't have decisions. I'm grateful for options. While I trust the process to gain clarity, I seek and wait for His PAT answer. Seeking and waiting *is* part of the process.

Praying And Trusting in the Fully Rely On God (FROG) blog, Christina

SOME OF LIFE'S BEST COLORS ARE BLACK AND WHITE

A friend's fifth grade son recently received news that he is color blind. Rose (name changed) discussed the world's analysis of this less-than-colorful diagnosis. She struggled with her grim response to the test results, while the rest of her family approached this news as a simple twist in their lives.

Interestingly, her son's teacher is also color blind. Perhaps this was part of God's plan to help navigate the family's course of action. Rose sought hope in this organic alignment between teacher and student. She appreciated how that specific vision test wouldn't have been on their radar if Jacob's (name changed) teacher hadn't shared his story about adapting to color blindness.

I wanted to support Rose without giving the impression that her son's diagnosis was a weakness. When someone hits a slippery slope in life, I handwrite cards, bake, or make tie quilts as my outreach default. Knowing that her son's favorite treat is brownies, I decided to bake a pan for this family.

As I stirred the fudgy concoction, I added crushed Oreos and thought about Jacob and his family as they navigated life's effects of color blindness. I looked into the mixing bowl as I watched chocolate batter blend with the Oreos. I saw black and white.

To my eyes, there were "only" two colors, but lack of color options didn't detract from the soon-to-be sweetness. The batter would need to endure the oven process to achieve delicious end results. The only way to transform that runny batter into formed gooeyness was through heat. Rose's family will be challenged with this new color wheel yet they face it *together*. Individual ingredients mixed to create one colorful unity.

A prism of light lifted my heart. Through grateful tears of a reassuring presence for this family, I saw that despite muted human perspective, life can become every vibrant color. I can paint my day from a full palette, adding new shades to my heart's canvas if I open the windows to invite lighter tones.

Cookies and cream brownies. Baby zebras. Flower, the skunk from Disney's *Bambi*. Pages from a captivating book.

Some of the best things on the lily pad are in black and white, Christina

ADMIRING THE MAKEOVER

Change is perpetual motion. At every moment, in all parts of the universe, transitions occur. Some shifts are dramatic, other evolutions are subtle.

I've been harvesting a bounty of professional changes since July. Without listing a bumper crop of examples, various fields where I've planted seed have been fruitful. I've also stumbled across bad apples in my orchards (i.e. daily mission fields).

Prior to this onslaught of adjustments, I did not consider myself naturally resilient. People define me as reliable, trusting me to start and complete what I say I'll do. The flip side of those characteristics can sometimes shackle me to a routine or relationship even if it no longer meshes with other dynamics.

As trees prepare to turn color, I appreciate their flexibility in the face of changing circumstances. They don't resist nature's process or create back-up plans to avoid or delay the autumn season. The leaves move with life's flow and adjust to their present conditions. Ironically, I'm eager to drive numerous miles to watch leaves transform but sometimes want to run like the wind when agenda deviations cross my lane of traffic. I think it's remarkable when others get out of their comfort zone, but I'm not always quite so eager to do this myself!

I've been in an extended stretch of frequent modifications. Instead of shriveling up like a fallen leaf searching for cover, I'm adapting to celebrate new colors. I'm reaping fresh energy across this latest yield.

Leaping from a camouflaged lily pad into vibrantly cultivated fields, Christina

BABY SIMBA

The lesson I learned in the FROG blog came from the movie *Lion King*.

Gratefully, my lily pad is waterproof as I watch a steady flow of raindrops outside. My thoughts match the perpetual motion of the rain, nearly flooding with fresh brainstorms. I've claimed 2018 as our family's year of restoration. I hooked Joel 2 and Hab. 2:1-3 as my scriptural anchors onto my annual growth plan.

Puddle jumping living and shallow water is being traded for bigger wave exploration. I have a tsunami of creativity and yearn to swim at an Olympic level instead of dog paddling. However, there is an undercurrent and my think tank has become shark infested. How do I temper this inventive energy while respecting the building process of each inspiration? This is where I picture myself as baby Simba in the Lion King story.

Baby Simba is filled with wonder and enough spunk to overpower a lion herd with his grandiose plans. He confidently sings about not being able to wait until he's king until Zazu, a seasoned hornbill, reminds him of learning curves. Simba's daddy, Mufasa, pours wisdom into his zealous son. Rafiki, the wise mandrill, advises Simba to look harder, to look beyond "see level."

Like Simba, I quickly switch to high gear and imagine countless opportunities to sail unchartered waters. I want to jump from the pond into the ocean, bypassing creeks, streams, or rivers to get there. I throw myself a mental life preserver (and some arm floaties) to capture my driftwood of thoughts.

Baby Simba's zest is blissfully contagious though it's Mufasa, Zazu, and Rafiki who wisely tether this baby feline to honor the circle of life. Like Simba, I must trust God's alignment and timing to sometimes hold me back from facing potential hyenas before I am ready for them. Mufasa, Zazu,and Rafiki are to Simba as the Father, Son, and Holy Spirit are to me.

I have much enthusiasm. I have much potential. I have much to learn. With faith in God's kingdom plan, I can jump into this day singing Hakuna Matata. No more worries for the rest of my days.

Like Rafiki on Lion King, I look harder into the reflective pool of the FROG Blog, Christina

FLYING SHOTGUN

With a forty-minute job commute, the drive invites 2400 seconds of uninterrupted thought space. Sometimes the time includes toggling between music stations. Other days, I listen to a podcast sermon. (To a frog, it's a 'padcast'). Occasionally I have abundant prayer needs, other times gratitude rolls off my tongue as quickly as my tires rotate toward the job site.

Yesterday morning, my mind retaliated against the peace I was trying to capture. There was a strong unsettling mood that threatened, 'I crave to be rebellious and ornery for no understandable reason.' I'm usually able to pinpoint a source for underlying tension. I typically work my way out of a funk by walking outside, listing positive options, or singing loudly to favorite songs. The Terri Clark song, *I Just Want to be Mad for Awhile* mocked my attempt to wrestle against this unexplainable irritation. These mind taunting needles burned a pirate tattoo in my spiritual skin.

The heaviness was unwelcome, yet something in me relished being cantankerous. As I neared my workplace, I knew I needed to trade in my crabby pants for a pair of professional britches. Through the windshield, mid-eye roll, I caught a glimpse of three large gulls flying in a triangle. They looked like a feathered trinity aimed straight toward me. I chuckled at the 'planted wink' flying overhead. Before I could say, "Thank you Lord for reminding me to fix my eyes on things above," a smaller bird flew out of nowhere. If that little flying trailer had a caption above his head, his bubble cloud may have read, "Father, Son, and Holy Spirit! Wait for me! I'll board Your flight!"

Among my dive-bombing thoughts and clouds of immaturity, those soaring gulls reminded me to fly above the buzzards of my mind.

Trading in turkey vulture feathers for a headdress among the Spirit in the Sky, Christina

EXPLORATIVE HEART SURGERY

Easter is one week from today and freshness blankets the lily pad of the FROG blog.

When I came out of the tomb (aka: my bedroom) this morning, I had a fleeting desire to go back 2000 years with a front row seat outside the cave where Jesus resurrected. Three days prior, on Good Friday, the world assumed Jesus' tomb would be His final resting spot. God had other plans for that rock Easter Sunday.

I'm curious to picture Jesus Easter morning, the day of his Resurrection. Did He easily roll the stone away from the cave entrance and step out? Did He walk through the rock? What was Jesus' facial expression? Wonder? Elation? Was His Resurrection peacefully tempered or was there a pointed energy burst? Were there animals nearby to witness this? None of the answers to these questions will get me into heaven, nor will the answers keep me out of heaven. I'm simply energized by mentally coloring outside of the lines.

Based on scripture, I read that Mary Magdalene was the first person at the burial site, but she gave limited details of the Resurrection. I can imagine she was too awestruck to write a detailed account of an event that profound. Whether Jesus departed from the tomb via feet or spirit, only God was (and is!) alive to answer that question.

Some of my greatest joys generate from stretching my imagination. I ask questions that some people define as blatant randomness. I thrive on "what if" conversations that encourage a mind to think beyond the horizon. I appreciate answers that educate. I applaud responses which don't invoke a need to prove or critically debate every question.

With a purely explorative heart, I leap into the pond of childlike fascination, Christina

ROADSIDE SIGN LANGUAGE

I drove past churches this week and their marquees advertise Palm Sunday, Passover, Maundy Thursday and Easter celebrations. Palm Sunday commemorates the day Jesus Christ entered Jerusalem as Messiah. The name Palm Sunday derived from the palm branches Jewish people waved at Jesus and laid in front of Him. Within days of that joyful procession, some of the same people who welcomed Jesus would demand His execution because he wouldn't conform to their beliefs.

The palms of Palm Sunday refer to branches. I picture the palms of my hands. I'm a morning person so I begin most days with a spirit of my palms waving in the air. I rejoice at the quiet victory as daylight stretches from its dark slumber. My palms are open to being generous, eagerly surrendering to God's plan for the upcoming journey.

Sometimes as a twenty-four-hour journey continues, I respond with a similar fickleness to which the Jewish people displayed after the palm branches had been withered and trampled. My palms which were originally wide open with anticipation and willingness become more shriveled and tight-fisted. My palm at dawn threatens to morph into a virtual face-slap by dusk. When I hit daily speed bumps, that same palm that high-fived the morning transforms into a "back off/talk to the hand" symbol by evening (sometimes much earlier)!

I share this personal accountability challenge to align my words and actions. When the 'donkeys' of my day flatten the lively palms, will I still offer open hands? When virtual poison ivy leaves cover my path instead of palm branches, will I still open my arms to welcome people and learning situations?

A frog uses sticky pads on its' feet to climb. From the FROG blog, when I handle rugged terrain I will strive to engage sticky webbed feet to my faith.

With more open palms (not limited to only one Sunday), Christina

A WATERED DOWN FORETASTE

It's the Monday before Easter. In organizing my day, I think of Jesus preparing for Holy Week. He'd have unlimited Mondays *after* His resurrection, but He was about to experience his last Monday in human form on earth. Based on what is listed on my calendar, I have some ideas about how my week may unfold. There is much of this week left to circumstances, conversations, and situations which I cannot foresee today.

What about Jesus? He knew what His week was going to look like. He knew His Friday would result in being teased, beaten, whipped, stripped naked and nailed with spikes to a tree in front of a crowd. I'm struggling to picture myself facing any *one* of those pains. Though Jesus knew His Good Friday would ultimately end in a Resurrection, I'm hard pressed to imagine His response when He woke up Monday morning with the week that He had ahead of Him.

Originally, I wrote a comparative message for today's FROG blog. The first draft discussed how my anticipation, hopes, worries, and weekly agenda paled compared to Jesus' Holy Week. The tone was meant to shed new light on general Monday woes. I realize my foolish speculation in attempting such comparison between my path and Jesus' path. I wasn't there. I cannot fathom knowing that absolutely no part of Him was spared from the upcoming send-off the world would give Him.

I'm abbreviating today's reflection from the FROG Blog with an invitation to try to fully capture what *may* have gone through Jesus' mind. What weighted His heart during His final week on earth? He dove deep into horrific pain to rescue me from drowning in sin's shallow waters.

With extreme gratefulness that *anything* in store for me will unlikely resemble what Jesus endured Good Friday, Christina

EASTER SEASON FRIENDS

Good Friday! I sent a few Easter cards this week and just finished one to a forty (plus) year friend. Allisa and I met in grade school and have swum life's lazy river lily pads *and* whitewater rafting currents. During Easter fasting, praying, and preparation, I realize she is a three-day Easter friend.

Allisa and I have faced Good Fridays: situational crosses, carrying heart burdens up steep hills, being 'Veronica' to wipe each other's tears, pulling thorns from our crown of dreams. We've spent Holy Saturdays waiting for understanding, reconciliation, bitter stings from Good Fridays to be healed with balm. We've graciously celebrated Easter Sunday's mountaintop vistas, brighter light, resurrected openings after dark dank boulders have moved.

Out of the Easter Triduum, I've learned a few lessons about Holy Saturday. Ironically, a Saturday season is when I've learned the most. There's no way I can wrap my FROG legs around the intensity of Good Friday. In my Good Friday-like moments, I identify with the fight or flight experience. I comprehend pain. It's tangible. It's in my face.

I can't fully fathom Easter morning until I get to heaven and see this from God's perspective. I've been blessed with times of extreme hope, wisdom, joy, supernatural peace. Those resurrection moments propel me. I bask in the intense light of spiritual soaring. Like Good Friday, Easter moments are tangible. They're in my face.

However, smack dab in the middle of crucifixion and resurrection is Saturday. How do I paddle in that seemingly lukewarm body of water? There's nothing to see per se beyond a memory of past and hope for the future. What about pain in the night but joy comes in the morning? (Ps. 30:5). What happens when morning after morning I wake with no sign whatsoever of joy? What do I do with the hangover of pain? How do I remain hopeful as I strain my bruised neck from Friday to anticipate Sunday? What about a waiting period that expands from doorstep to door*stop?* Whether I feel like it or not, I rely on the promise from Hab. 2:3 during Holy Saturdays: "For the revelation awaits an appointed time; it speaks of the end and will not prove false. Though it lingers, wait for it; it will certainly come and will not delay."

Allisa and I are like Easter perennials in a trifecta of soil. We've been repeatedly tilled, habitually planted, and gratefully harvested. I pray you have or will find an all-season porch friend in your spiritual Easter basket today!

Lessons and blessins from a three-leaf lily pad, Christina

WARNING: DON'T READ PAST THE FINE PRINT

There's a glare of jaded reflection off the lily pad this morning. I've had a disturbing behavior pattern that has increased in frequency and today I'm calling it out.

I'm compelled to encourage myself and readers through experiences where I believe I've made headway. By no means have I perfected each lesson, but lately within minutes or hours of posting the FROG blog, I am ferociously up close and personal living that message. I'm learning how deeper inspiration is drawn more from lost seas than river banks. The FROG blog would be easier to write on a lazy river than in waterfall rapids. Paddling forward...

Yesterday I discussed Easter friends, focusing on Holy Saturday. I'm on the tail end of a Holy Saturday job phase. With three months left on the contract, I wrote yesterday's blog from a spirit of optimism with light at the end of a job tunnel. Within twenty-four hours of that posting, I spiritually collided with a virtual wailing and gnashing of teeth. (*The rest of today's pep talk is for my eyes only. Should you comment on today's FROG blog, I'll know I'm in good company when it comes to missing the fine print* ☺).

I know I've been called, led, and prodded to said contract. My skill set includes finishing what I begin so I was hired to bridge unity between this project's beginning and end. I'm nearing the final phase of a fourteen-month contract. The original undertaking resembled a swinging bridge. The intensifying assignment requires fastening the swinging bridge to a hilly incline. Instead of hunkering into the final leg of this project, I'm chopping myself off at the knees by calculating hours until completion. I'm wasting energy *avoiding* suffering instead of recycling my uncomfortable edginess into useful productivity.

Here's the rub. I encourage weight loss clients toward their desired goal weight, but I'm currently tempted to shortcut through policy development. I coach high school students who want to quit before their team season is over, yet I struggle with completing staff evaluations. I convince my husband to finish our Scrabble match when his last letter draw is a Q with no U, but my own desk is spattered with partially written letters. As a contracted bridge builder, I need to stop mentally burning bridges and connect the canyon between this threatening mediocrity and excellence.

Yesterday I was planted firmly on my personal growth ladder. Today my trellis got knocked down. I reach for my *Easter Friends* blog, reread the wisdom from 'that author' and repeat Hab. 2:3. "For the revelation awaits an appointed time; it speaks of the end and will not prove false. Though it lingers, wait for it; it will certainly come and will not delay."

Striving to grow from tadpole to full grown FROG, Christina

PLEASE STEAL MY SHOW!

Talk about a spoiler alert during this morning's quiet time! God showed up in the FROG blog with His original feature presentation. It was an unplugged "Live from Heaven" highlight. No opening band and no messages from His show sponsors. He stepped into the spotlight and from the front row, I watched God's true story with 3D glasses.

Prior to God's stage presence, I had been watching a home movie in my mental theatre. My feature film starred antagonist Sir Borrow Tomorrow's Troubles. Supporting antagonizing characters included Lack of Clarity and Seventy-Two-Hour-Demand-on-a-Twenty-Four-Hour-Fuse (stars sometimes love many name hyphens).

Physically I was quiet in my "prayer theatre" but my internal volume resembled a metal band musical. I rocked to lamentations and was head banging from the front row of my mind. I was in surround sound, jamming to every angle of my situational analysis. I was mid-song when suddenly the sound system blew, and I remembered a 'random' lyric, (ahem) scripture.

"Here on earth you will have many trials and sorrows. But take heart, because I have overcome the world." (John 16:33, NLT). I'm not sure if God uses the word duh, but it was simply an obvious message. I recalled the scripture passage but in my sludge through swamp waters, I found the trials and sorrows reminder annoying. I was already in a heart burn state. The 's' after trial and sorrow became a salt shaker on a new skin graft.

Gratefully I didn't leave my prayer theater in a snit after scripture's first scene about testing and tribulations. "Take heart" (*knock it off,*

34

pay attention, chill out, be quiet, stop thinking long enough to hear God's voice over your own, Christina Eder's amplified translation 365:7-24). "I have overcome the world." *Have* overcome. Past tense. Scripture doesn't say God *will* overcome the world after trials and tribulations. It assures readers He's been there, done that.

Worldly antagonists threaten and will threaten my peace. People and situations may take swipes at my confidence, stir chaos, or shoot verbal vomit bullets during this earthly screenplay. However, when this movie is over, I can walk out of the theater (aka earthly death) and realize The Director has carved victory into His script. He has already accomplished His perfect encore.

Writing this revelation is simple. To live it, John 16:33 remains on my "Watch again, Must See, Repeat Play" list. At the end of this earthly film, He'll get the girl. He'll get *this* girl. He has already won.

As one of His stage hands from the FROG blog, Christina

FIXATE VS FLOW

I'm blessed to be married to a Mr. Fix-It man. Tig is the first to admit he's not a handyman when it comes to home repairs. He's amazingly talented in gearhead operations including restoring and using frugality to enjoy motorsports on a shoestring budget. He excels in vehicle maintenance, spends endless hours researching car builds, and imparts innumerable statistics about nearly every engine. Tig is fearless in finding atypical ways to fabricate a solution. Mistakenly I once thought I complimented him on a garage endeavor by saying, "Amazing! You cobbled that project seamlessly together!" He amusingly but pointedly told me amateurs do cobble jobs, he *fabricated* this repair.

Considering all his qualities, we reached a wilted patch in our marital lily pad in the FROG blog. Figuratively, the wheels have fallen off from pieces of our individual lives and family's lives. We have been in tow truck and repair mode for many months. This long span of heavy fabrication has thrown a wrench into our marriage. We've allowed dirty air filter situations to put the brakes on our own relationship vehicle. We need a fresh water flush and marital tune-up.

I got a sunrise view from the lily pad this morning. Together we've faithfully scraped our knuckles and changed life's flats. We've been each other's pit crew and relied on our Crew Chief. Recently, in our weariness, we've changed gears and instead of centering on God's guidance to accelerate or brake, we grabbed the wheel. We had, and still have pure intentions to help each other through this construction zone but have not necessarily respected speed limits or lane deviations.

Tig and I slowly shifted our resilient flow to fixate. Our overall joy got eaten because we 'fix-ated'. To avoid further 'as-fix-iation' we realign love into our lifetime warranty. Instead of resembling bulldozers in a garden, we recognize the need to ride together on a tractor. As we sit side-by-side on this tractor of life, I trust Tig has already planned to fabricate a larger motor or louder exhaust system.

Joyfully coasting instead of fixing the pedal to the metal in four-wheel drive, Christina

REQUIRED VACATION

Sabbath Day! I consider it my 24-hour weekly vacation. I love how God included Sabbath Day as a "command" for His people to refrain from tilt-a-whirl living. He instructs us to honor Him as Creator one day every week. This week, I used Sunday to take an unexpected walking retreat.

We live in a town that offers plenty of sidewalks, quiet neighborhoods, sitting spaces, and parks. I'm reading *The One Thing* by Gary Keller. With the sunshine and breeze, I chose to be outside to dig deeper into the pages of this incredible read! I grabbed the book and my journal and walked to the pond behind our complex.

I found a bench in the most direct sunlight to read. I wondered if unknowingly I had morphed into some *Left Behind* series because it was 11:00, nobody was outside, breezes were gentle, and the atmosphere held a mysterious hush. Generally, this scenario is my heaven on earth. I felt unsettled because I've reluctantly grown accustomed to an arena of ring tones, loud talking, bleeps, and buzzes.

I read a few pages of *The One Thing* and left the bench intending to return home to crochet. Instead, I walked to the neighboring subdivision and sat at the gazebo. I continued reading and the chapter discussed forced willpower and needlessly trying to accomplish mind-over-matter. I got so excited about Gary Keller's teaching that I power walked home to tell my husband about these eureka insights! (To describe how *The One Thing* discoveries impacted me would require writing another book to explain this book).

Tig had already left for the swimming pool to work out his body kinks and back pains. Instead of being bummed that he wasn't home, I trekked to another nearby park gazebo and journaled about these newfound discoveries from the book. I wrote feverishly until I "emptied" my thought container. I walked to a nearby ballpark and sat on a bleacher to pan for more literary gold from *The One Thing* treasure chest.

This three-hour walk-and-read, walk-and-journal pattern nourished me until my stomach was empty, and my bladder was full. As I headed home to get a snack, water, and restroom break, I turned my face upward and thanked God for writing a weekly retreat into His commandments. I energetically accept His request!

Puddle jumping with joy to learn and live from the FROG Blog, Christina

ARMOR ALL

I woke in the middle of the night with a nervous stomach. I had a sense that something wasn't right, or a sizeable change was on the horizon. I couldn't define "it," so I prayed especially for our son who is on a job site that temporarily separates him from his family. I needed to pray and process through that uneasiness and was finally able to return to sleep until the alarm went off.

On my morning commute, I saw a motorcycle driver pull into a heavily congested intersection. He sat up straighter on the seat and tightened his legs around the motorcycle as he navigated through traffic. His helmet and heavy protective gear led me to wonder how often and consistent do I really armor myself as Eph 6:10-18 instructs? What if I armored myself every day as if I was driving a motorcycle instead of a Nissan Juke?

In my Juke, I don't need to drive with a helmet. I am surrounded by protective metal, airbags, new tires, seat belt, windshield, mirrors, and a handful of other safety features. All vehicle precautions have been added by the factory without my concern. I trust the vehicle inspections have been done and each worker equipped the car with necessary safeguards (and a radio!). The automotive workers have properly equipped my car, but I am responsible for correctly utilizing those safety features. Just like God has laid out the instructions for proper living in the Bible, it is my job to live it on a daily basis. My immediate focus is to be alert, use the wipers and lights as needed, and readjust the seat and mirrors to my height after my 6'2 husband drove the car.

Drivers of any vehicle are responsible for several pounds of moving metal on the roads, but motorcyclists assume more risks than a typical automobile driver. I want to believe that a motorcycle driver has a heightened awareness to remain attentive and suit up for his or her journey. A forgotten helmet, nonprotective clothing, or a burnt-out bike light will be a larger hazard for a motorcyclist than an auto driver.

Despite the emotional residue from this morning's awakening with anxiety, our Creator's truth is that He's gone before me and stands behind me. As I start this day with a virtual key in the ignition, how have I armored myself? To fear or not to fear this day's travels. That is no longer a question if I believe in my spiritual armor. The question is if I've taken responsibility to suit up for today's drive. Am I spiritually and mentally dressed as a motorcyclist in rush hour traffic, or am I showing up for the day casually armored like I'm driving in a sedan for a Sunday country drive?

With my helmet of salvation, belt of truth, breastplate of righteousness, sword of the Spirit, shield of faith, and feet shod in peace, Christina

A PIECE OF PEACE

I'm FROG blogging on the lily pad of a wave crashing ocean instead of a quiet back water. My spirit refuses to be calm.

Jesus assures me in scripture that He left His peace (John 14:27). Why am I not picking up what He already left? I'm emotionally leaving a set of new luggage at the baggage terminal. The genuine leather luggage set is stuffed with peace, but I settle and claim a tattered backpack of restlessness. I recognize I have given frequent traveler miles to distractions and missed my connecting flights with God.

I write this to expose the darkness that is attempting to overpower my peace. Instead of enjoying a generously prepared chicken platter with all the fixin's and dessert, I'm overlooking the joyous feast to partake in chaotic spiritual indigestion. It's equivalent to bypassing a buffet line to settle for a jar of dill pickles. Which piece of peace will I embrace?

With a blog the size of a tadpole but the weight of a full-grown bull frog, Christina

ADULTING LIKE A KINDERGARTNER

This morning, I may have looked like an adult impersonating a kindergartner on the first day of school. I was in my quiet time, distracted by uncertain and undone big-ticket items hanging over my head. The upcoming tasks made me feel like a fast bowling ball rolling on an unlevel wooden alley.

I got closer to the time of leaving for work and found myself stalling. I rationalized that my delays were a "good kind of stalling". It was respectable to read extra chapters from my bible and write more in my prayer journal. I became a frozen kindergartner clinging to my Father, not wanting to leave quiet time to face the many unknowns of life's classroom. It was as if I was saying, "Abba, Daddy, one more hug, one more reassurance that the day is going to be ok, one more plea not to leave me alone."

While I grow in my learning about God's constant presence, my head, heart, feelings, and actions are sometimes disconnected. God gave me a gentle underlying nudge to move into the day's mission. I have experienced countless times prior to this morning that once I make it out the front door, somehow my courage grows.

Unsteadily, I collected what I needed for the day. Instead of God rushing to tell me to act my age or grow up, He softly pushed me forward and encouraged me. It was as if He reminded me that I'm like one of His kindergartners. His spirit repeated that growing pains are to be anticipated but He tackles those learning curves with His students.

I've been created with roots and wings. Interesting dichotomy that we have roots to keep us grounded to His truth, but wings to go out and tackle the world. It's crucial to go to quiet time to learn. It's expected to leave quiet time to serve.

"You are of God, little children, and have overcome them, because He who is in you is greater than he who is in the world (1 John 4:4). Translate: "You're going to be ok daughter. We'll talk about what you learned after your school day."

Stepping onto my Professor's strong shoulders as I apply lessons from His Tutorial, Christina

WINNIE THE POOH AND BILLY GRAHAM

I'm reading the *Tao of Pooh* by Benjamin Hoff. A friend loaned it to me with a suggestion to pay attention to people showing up for life through the characters of Pooh, Piglet, Tigger, or Rabbit. As an animal lover, I was eager to learn more from our furry companions. The book confirmed a simple but firm observation from a mentor, "Christina, you're trying too hard. You're complicating life. Just let it happen."

The excerpt from *Tao of Pooh* that stood out: "When we learn to work with our own Inner Nature and with the natural laws operating around us, we reach the level of Wu Wei. Then we work with the natural order of things and operate on the principle of minimal effort. Since the natural world follows that principle, it does not make mistakes. Mistakes are made--or imagined--by man, the creature with the overloaded Brain who separates himself from the supporting network of natural laws by interfering and trying too hard."

In a dialogue with Pooh, the author teaches how Tao doesn't force or interfere with flow. Instead, Tao allows life to work in its own way, organically producing results. I read *Tao of Pooh* during a work break and after work, I paged through a *Decision* magazine. "The Time is Short" article featured an interview with Billy Graham who said, ..."There are billions and billions and billions of planets and stars. And as far as we know, this is the only planet in *rebellion* against God."

Ouch! Rebellion? Ouch! Going outside of what my Creator crafted in His blueprint for my life? I never expected a connecting message between Winnie the Pooh and Billy Graham. A mentor's insight, the *Tao of Pooh*, and Billy Graham's interview in one day invited me to consider what I am filling and flushing out of the purity of life. I am discovering that any unrest and chaos is generated from living *my* will, (not *Thy* will) be done!

Seeking ponds to soak and flow without artificial coloring or (self) preservatives, Christina

BIGFOOT

This morning I saw a bumper sticker on the back of a car window that read, "Bigfoot doesn't believe in you either." I laughed at this comic relief among school zone congestion.

When I got past the bottleneck traffic I thought more about that Bigfoot bumper sticker. What if the word Bigfoot was substituted with Creator or God? How would I respond if the sticker read, "The universe's Creator doesn't believe in you either?"

I'd like to lead readers to hike around several vantage points. The explorative trails of thought involve big and small footpaths, all exceeding my 500-word limit on the FROG blog. Instead of putting my feet in two camps, I invite the reader to take a self-guided tour to explore their view around, "The universe's Creator doesn't believe in you either?"

With both feet in my Creator's camp, I leap from the lily pad, Christina

FORGIVENESS FESTIVAL

During a hot air balloon festival, I looked at the sky and in my mind's horizon, the word forgiveness elevated. I have a dream to ride in an untethered hot air balloon. I want the unbridled exhilaration of letting go and seeing where the winds (and pilot!) take me. Tethered to temporary constraints like schedule and finances, my balloon ride is delayed.

At the festival, I pictured climbing on board a brightly designed balloon. I didn't purchase an excursion ticket because my primary goal is to ride in an unrestrained balloon. The balloon owner promised to soar to several thousand feet, but I crave rootless abandon. I often live securely anchored to many things. Like this festival's balloon ride, I have opportunities to fly significant heights yet remain grounded to unseen safety chains (i.e. fears).

Sometimes unforgiveness looks like my tethered balloon. Hurt, resentment, and bitterness need to be indefinitely catapulted so why do I clutch strands of unforgiving rope? I *say* I forgive. I *think* I forgive, but under a ground cover, I'm still tethered to spiritual landfill. I don't allow hostility to completely release itself from my rocky ground. I fear I'm weak or lacking virtue if "forgive and forget" do not simultaneously occur.

I watched the festival balloons soar and there was magnificence combined with realization that they would rise only as far as the rope allowed. I notice when I untether my animosity, an inner vessel (forgiveness) rises and the size of painful memories fade. The forgiveness flight advances if I focus on the summit.

In piloting my soul's hot air balloon, I'm initially excited to launch forgiveness. If I don't see or feel immediate updraft effects, why do I quickly return to ground level to revisit the injuring situation? Inner tethers suppress me only if I tie myself to a burden, weight, or offense. Once forgiveness is intentionally untethered, I can still observe the balloon, but it's liberated from captivity. I can still acknowledge the balloon (offense) but its' magnitude shrinks.

When (sadly, sometimes if) I unshackle the tether, my balloon is freed to travel to new horizons without a ratty rope! I may still have memory of the 'combustible experience' but as freestyle forgiveness is unleashed, emotional deflation fades.

I use the FROG blog as public accountability to grow into forgiveness with an untethered hot air balloon mindset. I understand it may be natural to observe balloons (past disappointments). It's important to anticipate wind shifts instead of stuffing inclement weather patterns into the caverns of my soul. The journey to forgiveness has varying lengths of rope (time to heal).

Ultimately, the most invigorating part of the ride comes when the imprisoned shackle marries the joyous updrafts to transport it to a world of wide-open freedom. Forgiving is essential if I want a zenith view. It's time to let rope burns heal and loose the noose of resentments.

Seeking steady air flow and soaring toward the Only One I'm tethered to, Christina

RUNNING AHEAD OF TIME

I walked to the mailbox this morning and caught my mind racing through the upcoming day's agenda. In that 15 minutes to the mailbox and back, my stream of restless thinking took me from 5:45 *a.m.* real time to 10:00 *p.m* presumed visionary time. I hadn't even taken a shower, but my 16-hour assumed foresight added new meaning to running ahead of schedule!

I realized I permitted pre-worry to lead me into a tunnel of anxiety. Sometimes I spend more time avoiding a struggle, but this morning I allowed undisciplined thought patterns to tie my stomach in knots. My immediate mission was to tweak my mindset to envision the tremendous possibilities and surprise blessings God could reveal throughout the day. Mentally, I reverted back to the one breath I was guaranteed. 6:01 a.m. real time. I wrote a reasonable approach to talk myself down if (realistically, when) mindless mulling begins to shout.

My reality check pep talk from my journal:

"As SOON as you assume or anticipate the outcome of your next minute, hour, or day, stop. Ask:

-Will this situation, decision, or conversation get me into heaven or keep me out of heaven?

-Is anybody hurt or killed? (translate: no 911 call, no obituary, no problem)

-Praise or prayer? Fear can (and needs to) be converted to prayer; Joyful surprises translate to gratitude.

-Step toward or step away? Will "x" step me toward or away from my goal, dream, behavior change."

1 Cor. 2:9 backs up my proclamation with Truth: "But, as it is written, "What no eye has seen, nor ear heard, nor the heart of man imagined, what God has prepared for those who love him." Lord, help me (quickly) default to anticipation for whatever You have prepared for each nanosecond of this day.

Letting the FROG blog waters settle with simplicity, Christina

A $200K LESSON CAUGHT ON CAMERA

I heard a story about a woman who wanted a picture of herself at an art museum. She knelt in front of the exhibit to take a selfie and the back of her shoe bumped the art frame. The resulting domino effect led to $200,000 worth of exhibit damage. That photographer's museum admission ticket had suddenly escalated with a simple slip of her foot.

We all could share a story (or more) about accidents resulting in unanticipated costs. I can't imagine there was ill intent in this woman's heart when she sought to capture a photo memory of something that intrigued her. Her example reminds me of how self-absorbed I can be. I'm sometimes less aware of my surroundings and fellow journeymen than I want or need to be.

A proverbial snapshot of pride comes before the fall (from scripture's teaching in Prov. 16:18) brings me into focus. Even if I'm not taking physical selfies, my mental camera is sometimes stuck in self-video format. I stream events or situations where I flourished or wasn't recognized for what I deemed significant undertakings. Before long, I have produced a book series based around that one occurrence. A pastor uses a litmus test to determine self-centeredness. He asked, 'When you receive a group photo from an event you attended, who do you look for first in that photo?' Your answer reveals your egocentric levels."

What financial damage have I caused through accidental or intentional self-absorption? If time converted to money and my one-sided perceptions represented withdrawals, I'd risk bankruptcy. Like this museum photo bomb situation, how close or often has my foot (or words or thoughts) rested on a virtual pride rock? Each rock has potential to create significant landslides when I lose focus on others along my path.

From the pond of pure water living, I study my reflection and paddle away from self-righteous pride, Christina

SPIRITUAL REST STOPS

My work commute involves a 40-minute scenic drive along the Smoky Mountain foothills. I've grown accustomed to the roads, but never want to lose the wonder of those sunrises, lake views, rolling fog, or the occasional morning thunderstorms. Sometimes I battle tension from drivers weaving on a fast-paced mission (I jokingly figure they must be the most dedicated employees who enjoy their work enough to jeopardize other drivers by driving to their jobs so quickly).

Yesterday, I tuned in to how many churches are along the way. I concentrated on reading the church sign messages (as quickly as I could at 55 mph). One sign reminded readers to be of courage because the Lord goes before us. Another reminded "ye to taketh up your cross daily" in classic King James translation. A creative sign maker posted, "This church is a daily food distribution center, delivering the bread of life." I also appreciated a marquee's invitation, "Come camp out in God's tent for 'smore of Jesus." A smaller rural church proclaimed, "Now open Sundays!"

Whether those sign messages had been recently changed or my eyes were directed in a new way, they provided spiritual rest stops. Uplifting words elevated my spirit after a long work week. I gave a quick shout out for the people who taught me to read. I would have missed those advertised energy boosts if teachers had sped past me without stopping to teach me to read.

Leaping with gratitude for authors, teachers, and church sign hangers in our carpool world, Christina

OVERNIGHT RETREAT, A POTENTIAL OXYMORON

Last week, our youth group was preparing for a mission trip. Part of the middle school training events included an overnight retreat. Our campus is nestled in a campground-like setting so for most students, the grounds were familiar and close to home.

Familiarity didn't quell the concerns for some students who protested the overnight training. The director explained the benefits of overnight attendance, but two students persisted with a counter offer. They proposed staying until 10:30, go home to sleep, and return at 7:00 the next morning. The director maintained mandatory overnight attendance.

One of those two students looked disappointed about staying overnight, but quietly resigned. The other one wasn't giving up. She bargained to return to campus at 6:30, a half hour before camper wake-up call. She offered to make breakfast for the teammates. The decision was set. Unless there was a doctor related or medical reason, overnight participation was vital.

I related to this girl's pain because in middle and high school, I enjoyed being invited to parties, but when it involved a sleepover, it was no longer a party to me. I reached social overload by 10:00 and wanted to be home. Acceptance from peers was important to me, but the intense need for space eclipsed the light of the party.

With mustered courage, I approached this girl when she was walking away. I shared my experience about overnights away from home and asked if she could relate. She nodded and gushed a wind of response, "Yes!" I continued, "Does it sound silly that I'm an adult and *still* feel like a sixth-grader at a sleepover when I have work-related overnight attendance?" She laughed with relieved understanding and enthusiastically responded, "No!"

That vulnerable one-on-one admission led her to open her heart. She talked about how she enjoyed friends, shared meals, campfires, and talking. She said she could force herself to play icebreaker games even though she thought they were a childish time waster. The pressure came when she needed to disengage from the crowd. She not only wanted, but needed, quiet and space for soul restoration.

For some, when continual interaction is expected, community building can invite wall building. There are benefits to extended interaction when groups are newly created or need reinforcement. Respect is often a team building goal, but lack of respect for someone's personal threshold can erode the original well-intentioned purpose. Requiring people to prolong shared space can generate a forced connection, possibly resulting in disconnection.

Community is important, team building is necessary, networking is crucial, stretching beyond our comfort zones invites strength. I value those advantages and it's equally critical to value the beauty of reasonable margins of restoration. With some gentle tweaks in the world's stopwatch regime, a quiet sensitive person can embrace interaction without flailing a white flag of weary surrender.

With restful peace from a quiet lily pad, Christina

NOT THE FULL TRUTH

The word 'actually' seems to be used more frequently in many conversations I've had lately. I'm not sure if 'actually' is a version of "like" (i.e. 'That play was so like amazing') or if I'm simply more aware of 'actually' being used as a clarifying filler. For example, when somebody explains what they mean, the person may say, "actually, the situation was more eventful than..." or "it was actually most frustrating because it was something you'd see when..."

In all actuality, I ponder another phrase from the lily pad of observations. "To be honest with you." I hear a version of this nearly every day, "This is what "x' is saying, but to be honest with you, I think..." Or abbreviated, "Honestly? I really think she should tell him..."

When did we incorporate honesty as a clarifying statement? When speaking, do we need to credit truth with a phrase or word that assures listeners or viewers we're being truthful? I tested a potential response I'd like to incorporate when someone says honestly. I tried this on a longtime friend who honestly has a great sense of humor and is truthful about feedback.

Speaker: "Honestly?"

Me: (mild interruption) "Yes, versus *dis*honestly." (insert a wink when the speaker understands the wit)

Or

Speaker: "She can do whatever she wants, but to be honest with you, I think she needs to..."

Me (after the honest person finishes their sentence): "Just so I know we're on the same page, you said she can do whatever she wants, but to be honest with you...,' When you said you were being honest with me, was there a dishonest version of this situation/conversation/opinion that you were going to share also?" (another wink and smile to indicate I'm not pontificating).

This friend cautioned me to only use this banter with discretion (translate: that could turn sideways in a hurry). I appreciate her honesty! I promise to tell the truth, the whole truth, and nothing but the truth. If there's truth but it won't add value or love to someone, I will honestly remain silent.

Seeking truth in love, Christina

VIOLENCE AND VICTORY

I'm reading Pastor Joel Osteen's book, *"You Can, You Will."*
Pastor Osteen wrote about fixing our minds on a positive default
setting. He used the example of a 2007 beauty pageant contestant
who slipped and fell as she walked across stage on her way to the
evening gown competition.

She was embarrassed, and the audience was unforgiving with their
laughs and humiliating comments. Despite this fall, the contestant
advanced to the top five for the next competition. Each contestant
was to draw a random question out of a hat and answer it. She was
asked, "If you could relive any moment of your life over again,
what event would you choose?" Instead of verbally stumbling from
her most recent fall just minutes before, she responded with her
(presumed) practiced answer: she'd go back to Africa to work at
the orphanage to see children's beautiful smiles and feel their hugs.

This story stuck with me because it revealed an area I need
practice. I challenge myself to embrace life's updrafts and
maneuver the down winds. Both are necessary for flight. When I
read stories from the Bible, victory over violence is featured.
David and Goliath's writer could have supplied graphic detail
about an intense search for the perfect sized stones to load David's
sling shot. Instead of concentrating on his projected sweat and
blood, the story highlights the win over Goliath.

Noah's Ark may have showcased the smelly animals and reminded
us that the oversized boat had no sanitary waste conditions. Instead
the story assures us that God is faithful to His people even after our
world floods. Jesus' birth isn't a documentary about Mary's labor
pains and delivery process. We read about what death by
crucifixion entails, but the Bible is slightly (and graciously) vague

about Jesus' cross. Biblical authors wrote victory into their climax. Those stories weren't sterile, yet authors didn't buy the tagline "if it bleeds, it leads." They chose to maximize the triumph.

I'm accepting Pastor Osteen's invitation to write and practice the highlights of my experiences. Some of my highlights came from my downfalls. None of our lives are wrinkle free, but we may have less worry lines when we give our focus a facelift. That inner beauty could reduce the fine, or not so fine lines.

Training myself to take in more light, so I can decrease the dark circles around my eyes, Christina

WRESTLE OR REST-LE

My lily pad floated into waters resembling a wrestling arena instead of a gentle pond. I'm looking ahead *for* God and simultaneously resisting the urge to jump ahead *of* God. (Humbling confession: why do I look for God *anywhere* if I act upon my belief that He is eternally present?). What adds muscular weight to this wrestling match is that I comprehend I need these currently abrasive lessons for future assignments. No part of my natural fiber wants to face 'Patience, the Woman Eating Giant' in any arena!

Cross training (more cross than training) was bulking my character this morning when I read, "Blessed are the peacemakers." Peace maker, not peace taker. There is chaos and growing pains in my job assignment, yet the devotional teaching reminded me to be a peace *maker*. I want to fight this learning curve irritant, but God is calling me to rest (le) in a more surrendered pattern. He is the Coach, the Referee, the Cheering Audience of my wrestling and rest(ling) match.

Sometimes in spiritual circles, a mentor will ask, "How is your walk?" This question refers to a level of connection with your Creator. I'd rather be asked about my *run* with the Lord. Maybe the quicker our pace, the quicker I can avoid this present suffering? What about, how does my *sprint* with the Lord look like? (Sometimes it seems more like a *scurry*).

It seems natural to build my endurance when running, yet when I read about longsuffering in Romans the spiritual terrain becomes more treacherous. " Not only that, but we rejoice in our sufferings, knowing that suffering produces endurance, and endurance produces character, and character produces hope, and hope does not put us to shame (thank God!), because God's love has been poured into our hearts through the Holy Spirit who has been given to us" (Roman 5:3-5).

I aspire to be salt of the earth, but not as willing to accept the high (blood) pressure that comes from *being* genuine salt. I'm feebly attempting to beat God's stopwatch in this round. I want a happy ending solution with less sweat equity than I'm willing to pour out. Through my black eye realization, I see I need to rest (le) more and wrestle less.

I'm not at the power walk stride that I desire, but God is pacing me to prevent torn hamstrings and cold muscle tears. Creator of endurance, make me quick to desire how You are guiding me through longsuffering. Grant me discernment between longsuffering caused by my errors and longsuffering caused by Your teaching illustration. Help me recognize that Your answer doesn't indicate *how* long the suffering may be. Instead of running from pain, remind me to rejoice and respect Your "Terms of Endure-ment."

In His stride of a resting FROG moment on the lily pad, Christina

TREAT MEANT

I often use Socrates' questioning method of teaching to encourage new answers to surface. As I mindfully floated on the lily pad today, I asked what the word treatment means to me? Dividing treatment into two parts, what examples do I associate with the word "treat?" What treats have I received that remain memorable? What treats have I given that generated unforgettable responses?

The dictionary defines treatment as "the act or manner or an instance of treating someone or something. The method in which it is handled." This definition allows ample room for several prospective treatment options. I return to Socrates' questioning style to dig deeper for ideas. What are the parameters I use to measure when I'm treating others how I want to be treated? Using examples of my treat desires (dark chocolate, candles, spiritually engaging conversations), do I gift others with their favorites? Does the energy I release toward others indicate a treat I'd like to receive?

I recently watched Marie Forleo interview Tim Ferriss who invited the audience to think about "treating others the way you want to be treated." Ferriss suggested an alternative consideration. He asked if you treat *yourself* the way you treat others? Do you speak to others the way you speak to yourself? Do you respect margins and display grace for yourself with the same frequency as you allow for others? Self-care often overflows to more easily support other people and activities.

Ferriss isn't promoting selfish love or self-serving treatment. He recommended viewers to practice compassion on themselves to experience what treating others kind-heartedly looks and feels like. He questioned how someone could understand what treating others thoughtfully looks like if they don't treat themselves with courtesy. I've experienced Ferriss's observations in my life. When I'm impatient or severe with myself, I struggle against irritability or harshness toward people and projects. When I speak slower and build larger margins between thoughts or schedules, I'm gentler with others.

To respect my 500-word FROG blog limit, I leave my lily pad to review more answers from my treatment plan. I hope you will invest time to discover what treat means to you. What is your treat-meant? To treat yourself, to treat others? I believe your answers will translate to upgraded treats!

Leaping with care, Christina

WHO WROTE THE BOOK OF LOVE?

I'm writing a historical collection for an 80-year old gentleman who wants to leave a legacy of family stories for his children. "Pappy" is perfectly healthy and said he wants to capture recollections while his memory is sharp. His tribute points to key people in his life, especially what he learned from his dedicated mother and WWI veteran father.

Pappy discussed how vital God has become but recognized his spiritual blindness sometimes prevented him from seeing much of God's viewpoint. Through these eight decades, God's teaching eclipsed Pappy's original perception and he strives to shine light into others' lives through a wiser lens. Our rich discussions led me to wonder how I would answer the questions I've asked Pappy. What will I impart to our son and granddaughters?

In my reflections, I haven't "read" the words from my book of life, but I picture an oversized catalog with colorful pages. In my mind's eye, the plot is printed in traditional black. The yellow highlighted parts mark the sections of my earthly journey that matched God's *original* storyline for my life. I'll be curious to find out how God transformed my missteps into greater strides for His glory. He uses every piece of my earthly journey to bring His vision into better than Blu-Ray definition. (Knowing that God doesn't waste any of my 'trashy moves' reassures me that we both support recycling)!

When I've stepped out of His script or allowed the enemy to kill, steal, and destroy, those sentences are edited through His grace and forgiveness filter. All colors that lead up to the final chapter are important. However, the main climax of His story will be fully revealed at the end with His credits rolling in black, yellow, and every hue that painted my life.

I picture a colorful encore with plenty of victorious pink representing joy. I imagine an abundant section of vibrant green reminding me of new life. Ample paragraphs of purple showcase His loyalty. Royal blue, blood reds, white purity, silver wisdom, genuine gold.

No matter what shades of the past or rays of a bright future, He will get the girl. He's already won this girl! Thank you to Pappy and all other wise mentors who have colorfully decorated my path.

Smiling with highlights from a bright green lily pad, Christina

CHEVRONS

My Mom taught me to crochet when I was in elementary school. We began with single crochet chaining, double crochet stitches, and eventually created more elaborate patterns. In her crafting projects, Mom gravitated toward chevron patterns. Her blanket colors and sizes were different, but Mom's handiwork often displayed her signature "V" stitch.

I remember Mom looking peaceful when she crocheted. I'd sit on the couch beside her and pull yarn from the skein at a pace to match her stitching flow. Her hands moved rapidly but she was silent other than quietly repeating patterns in a definitive tempo style. Her chevron "cadence" was, "ten crochet up, top the peak with three doubles, chain one, top the next peak with three doubles, and head back down the V with ten double crochets."

As I became more skilled in crocheting, Mom used yarn patterns to teach life lessons. Using the chevron shape, she taught about life's ups and downs. A crocheted mountain requires counting to ten when stitching up *and* down. Both sides of the mountain are vital because each offer a different view of the tapestry. At the chevron points, there's a double trinity and to finish the blanket with excellence, you cannot stop at the top or bottom of the "V".

I watched Mom rip out several rows of a project because she made a significant error in her pattern's foundation. She told me how one additional or missed stitch creates an off-centered blanket. I learned the importance of counting stitches and fixing a mistake as soon as you find it.

It took me one difficult lesson of not heeding her instruction. I figured with two extra stitches, I could drop one on each side, so the end number remained the same. Instead of correcting my work at that point of miscalculation, I moved forward. My first chevron afghan turned into a V shaped blanket with a small base and large fanned out top. Crocheting, as in life, is seeing how an unfixed mistake can expand and "unravel" over time.

Mom taught that when working with darker colored yarn (i.e. life's valleys) stitches sometimes needed to be pulled gently apart for visual clarity. She adjusted to lighting limitations by using daytime to crochet dark colors and evening hours to crochet brighter hues. She taught me to relax if I didn't see a pattern take shape until several rows were completed. She'd gently repeat, "Just keep working through it. Don't worry about future stitches, you can only crochet one stitch at a time."

When I start any crochet project, I still "hear" Mom's reassurance about weaving shape into my life tapestry. Foundations are vital, all colors matter, each stitch counts, all details make a difference to the Creator.

Casting a life hook and line from my crochet and pray lily pad, Christina

VINTAGE BOUTIQUES

My quest this week is to use word changes to reframe my perspective. For example, instead of setting "good" or "bad" limitations, I'm upgrading the words good with great and bad with different. This practice is a spin-off from last week's personal challenge of embracing and appreciating plans beyond my Option A.

When an interaction doesn't fit within *my* parameters, I'm choosing to filter my response as, 'different than my original expectation'. When life works well (according to me), I draw fresh energy from acknowledging a specific interaction as great or excellent instead of settling for a good. I often find that "different from my original expectation" is a good thing if God is involved in the "different".

I experimented using this verbal makeover with my mother-in-law. She was discussing her assisted living housing and said she is relieved not to be in a nursing home. I value stories from older people and agree with the person who quipped that when an elderly person passes, it's like one library burning down. I asked my mother-in-law how she thought people would respond if nursing homes were called antique galleries? Or perhaps, vintage boutiques? She humored me with a hearty laugh and wished me good luck to convince a universal switch to define nursing homes as antique malls.

Leaping into a great day that has potential to show up differently than my Plan A, Christina

A LADY OF LEISURE

Sometimes when someone experiences a cluster of mishaps, I hear the quip, "Well, "it" comes in threes, what's next?" From what vantage point does "it" refer? This morning, "it" came in threes. The "it" was a song, a devotional, and a recall from Billy Graham. I write the *FROG blog* in my Martha and Mary Studio, named as a reminder to learn *and* live, to balance sitting with serving.

During this morning's walk I hummed a song in which I remember only one line, "To walk humbly with God." It played in my mind as I prepared for the day. To walk with God, I must be humble. (If I'm not humble when walking with the Creator of the Universe, I might want to check to see who I am *really* walking with)!

One line from my morning devotional grabbed my attention. "A leisurely pace accomplishes more than hurried striving" *(Jesus Calling,* Sarah Young,*).* I recalled Billy Graham's advice from when he was interviewed toward the end of his earthly life. Paraphrased, Graham told the interviewer that if he were to live his life over, he would use a 3-1 ratio of ministry. He'd spend three years preparing, learning, and studying, followed by one year of public preaching.

Graham shared his acquired wisdom of a 3-1 evangelizing cycle in the *Christianity Today* article "*What I Would Have Done Differently*," compiled by Collin Hansen. Graham said, "One of my great regrets is that I have not studied enough. I wish I had studied more and preached less. People have pressured me into speaking to groups when I should have been studying and preparing. Donald Barnhouse said that if he knew the Lord was coming in three years he would spend two of them studying and one preaching. I'm trying to make it up."

From a worldly definition, a lady of leisure often means to be financially independent, not requiring employment for life's expenses. Walking forward, I want to be a lady of leisurely pace. To walk humbly with God.

To walk (not run, but movement is necessary).

Humbly (with subordination).

With (not ahead, not behind, not pulling or dragging).

God (He is the Grand Finale, the last word of one song line singing volumes of understanding).

With three-fold appreciation from the FROG blog, Christina

GHOSTS?

My husband and I took a three-day vacation to celebrate our 25-year wedding anniversary. I emptied the suitcase we use as our granddaughter's craft and toy box, so I could pack for our trip.

When Tig and I got to the cabin, I told him how odd it seemed to see our suitcase filled with clothes vs. Marley Mae's toys, books, and craft supplies. Same container, different purpose.

I unpacked and found a lone cookie cutter which Marley Mae uses for tracing designs on paper. The cookie cutter was a sweet touch to have a piece of her artistic spirit with us. Again, same object, different use.

I pulled the cookie cutter out of the suitcase to show Tig this forgotten gem. He smiled and said, "An angel came with us." He saw a cookie cutter angel. Marley draws ghosts from that same cookie cutter. Same object, different view.

Seeing a FROG blog sunrise under a new light, Christina

GIVE AND TAKE

Reality check! The promises we make in dating compared to the vows we keep in marriage can be significantly different. When I finish laughing after reading that blatantly obvious statement I'll reflect among the algae around my lily pad.

This follow through of promises isn't limited to marriage and dating. In business, small groups, and schoolmates, early stages of relationships lean toward a (nearly) natural willingness to share time, space, possessions, ideas, chores, or money. As the relationships progress, sometimes the give and take appears to look like more giving than taking. Both parties hopefully presume that each is to give 100%. Some days, the pendulum shifts to 80/20. Some seasons challenge us to give 90% and take 10%. When we come face-to-face with our self-centered-chops' licking-monster, we may believe our give and take ratio is nearly 99-1%.

Give and take. 50-50. Two to tango. I get that. Dating give and take could mean giving love notes, taking flowers. Giving compliments, taking kisses. Giving surprise coffee invitations, taking time to listen intently to one another's heart. Offering dreams to share together, receiving tickets to achieve some of those dreams.

During Tig and my 25-year marriage (and counting!), we vowed for better or worse. What about best and worst? In sickness and in health. At the altar, we hear sickness and may envision headaches and stuffy noses. What if sickness includes an amputated limb or a stroke? The meaning of give and take drastically shifts. Giving rides to therapy. Taking a spouse's sudden mood swings. Giving sharp words. Receiving no apologies. Giving smiles across a hospital room. Taking a squeeze of their hand as our only thanks.

When relationship scales are tipped (according to our vision), some people fight fire with fire. At times, I've taken to fighting ice with ice. My grace and mercy thermometer registers below zero with a wind chill factor blowing from the north. My attitude goes south, and I need to be exposed to a sunnier disposition.

I challenge all people, *especially* the one sitting at this keyboard, to consider relationships as investing and accepting. Sometimes our investment to honor another's requests yields a high rate of return. We may receive gratitude or reciprocal giving. Sometimes another person's investment into what appeals to us lends itself to our greater return.

May I increase my grateful acceptance for all investments from others who add value to my life. Remind me to spend more energy applauding others instead of calculating selfish rates of return.

With an APR of 100% in and out of the FROG blog, Christina

SIFT

I implemented a practice of selecting one word annually to develop virtue in an area I felt weak. Last year I chose PUSH (Persevere/Pray Until Something Happens). The year of PUSH-ing produced an overdue birth after a pregnant spiritual desert. During that year of exercised persistence, I became enlivened with intense desire to take big bites from life's buffet of delicious options.

I experienced an almost unrealistic zeal stemming from release of old thought and behavior patterns. Before an untamed spirit could overpower my resources, I tempered my energy to claim SIFT as this year's focus. My husband calls my sifting process a "Love it or List it Year", adapted from HGTV's real estate show.

I discovered through the PUSH last year, I was persevering until *some*thing, *any*thing less painful than current circumstances, happened. I now realize I wasn't approaching suffering with an invitation to learn and grow. With a joyless heart and unclear mind, I wasn't receptive to lightened lessons taught from darkened experiences. I was pushing just to push in *any* direction. This year, I sift my beliefs and to what I commit. I sift how to spend time and money. I sift what words I speak and what I read. I sift which material possessions I really want to keep. I work toward processing through a gentler and kinder filter.

Sifting has been like putting my mind and soul (cabinets, closets, and file drawers) on a spiritual diet. I'm turning former weights into more useful muscle to free up my entire being. I understand there will be circumstances, personalities, and possessions that I'd rather "list" than love, but an increase in awareness *with action* has decreased much physical and mental disorganization.

SIFT-ing to develop a Greatest Hits Collection of my life on the lily pad, Christina

BELIEFS

I got to talk with a nearly 30-year old about living according to his beliefs and core values. He and I have different views about spiritual beliefs yet share incredible conversations about qualities we appreciate in humankind.

He was recapping an unexpected disappointment stemming from how he felt wrongfully treated. Mid-sentence he interjected, "I hope this conversation doesn't turn into a Jesus talk because I don't believe in all that God _____ (reader discretion)." Ordinarily, I would have encouraged his heart to be open to Christian practices, but I withheld my comments.

He may have mistaken my silence as not hearing his proclamation, so he repeated, "I'm serious. I *really* don't believe in God." I chose a neutral tone and responded, "OK." He pressed, "I know what you think, but I don't believe that way." I asked, "Do you *want* to believe in your Creator?" He answered no. I questioned why he continued to affirm what he *doesn't* believe. I asked him to talk about what he *does* believe.

Until recently, like this young man, I focused on differences between what I believed and what others believed. I saw communication gaps as canyons. I probably missed inspiring dialogue because my comparisons saw barriers instead of bridges to connect fellow explorers seeking life's value. I've come to realize how people and situations have more similarities than outlandish differences.

In one of her teachings, Christine Caine, founder of A21 Campaign and Propel Women, used a visual to show how our emphasis often becomes our truth. She projected an oversized white canvas with a picture of a tiny black dog on the far side of the screen. She asked the audience to vividly describe everything they saw on the screen. Unanimously, the tiny black dog stole the spotlight. Not one description mentioned the brightly lit screen that consumed nearly 95% of the stage.

Instead of summarizing my viewpoints, I've chosen to end today's FROG blog with reader challenge questions about his or her beliefs. Do we miss small features (like joys or warning signs) because we're consumed by a larger picture? Or do we presume there will be dark spots on every white canvas, so we spend energy adjusting or fixing the spots? Or perhaps we think if we care for every dark spot, eventually we create a blot-free screen from which to view life?

What foundational references do you use to create or debunk the creed you live? We can strengthen or weaken our original perception by challenging our primary reference point.

Believing my core values and trusting my Creator to supply updates for truth, Christina

DO YOU REALLY MEAN THAT?

From the mobile stage of my driver's seat, I belted out the tune, *Thy Will be Done.* I pretended to be Hillary Scott's (wanna-be) back-up vocalist and suddenly stopped mid-song. Hillary kept singing on the radio. I paused. Five minutes prior to that song, I started my morning commute with a synopsis of an upcoming conversation with my boss.

I hoped the pending job discussion would encourage my boss to "free me up to pursue career opportunities in other areas." I was secretly hoping she would agree that this contract was not a good fit for either of us. I struggled to open my mind and heart to *however* she'd respond.

The past three months of this job assignment has been a Mt. Rainier sort of climb and my heart has been a thick ice block. I spiritually slipped off my lily pad and fell into dank waters, surfacing in "toad mode" instead of "FROG jog". My Fully Rely On God living landed in quick sand.

During the commute, I discovered that I'm in a painful building phase of a contract that has left much debris. I want to sweep the sawdust out the door. I'd rather do some demo instead of renovating the blueprints of my expectations. Was I singing Thy will be done, but meaning *my* will be done?

While wading through this job's murky waters, I reach toward a dock of trust. I am swimming face-to-face with question marks: "Are my actions and spirit paddling toward the same Lighthouse?" "Do I *really* mean the words I sing from Hillary Scott's song?" "Does my conduct proclaim that my Creator's will is being done?"

I'm striving to willingly accept my Architect's blueprint for my life. Let me step with confidence in knowing that He is my guide,

79

even if I'm unable to see beyond grimy circumstances. I yearn to be a trust walker, not a trust toddler!

Sprouting in bountiful leaps from the anchored lily pad, Christina

RUDOLPH THE RED-NOSED REINDEER

From a statistical standpoint, I've learned how safety is frequently found in numbers. Those larger numbers could benefit some situations and they provide insurance against certain catastrophes, but are surpluses invested in the best or most necessary things?

I picture Rudolph the Red Nosed Reindeer. The story is crafted around the underdog (or perhaps 'under deer'). The little no-namer. We recall Rudolph, not *a* red nosed reindeer, not *another* red nose reindeer, but *the* red nosed reindeer. I'm hard pressed to recall the names of the other eight other reindeer, despite their strength in numbers.

Dasher, Dancer and reindeer crew were counted as the studs selected to pull Santa's sleigh. They represented safety and strength in numbers. They had each other's tails and antlers. Christmas Eve arrived, and a heavy fog threatened to shut down their overnight delivery service. No amount of brawn could safely carry a sleigh full of presents in the dark fog.

After what I imagine to be a powerful deer showdown for sleigh leader, Santa chose the least likely to be voted into the reindeer Ironman. He handpicked the one who wasn't allowed to play in any reindeer games. Rudolph was ridiculed for the beacon at the end of his nose. To the world of reindeer, Rudolph's nose may have been considered a disability. Santa needed the other eight deer as muscle power but carefully selected the reindeer who had a unique gift. Rudolph graduated from taillight to headlight status that Christmas Eve despite being originally uncounted in the numbers. . God seems to do the same thing. From our human perspective, He doesn't choose who seems to be best suited for a position.

I'm hopping onto Rudolph's back. I'll model his example to quietly and gently keep my nose lit. I ask God to use my beacon to cast brightness along the path where deliveries to the heart need to be made.

Seeking to be a strong fawn in His chosen team of Reign-deer!

Leaping from a lighted lily pad, Christina

WAR WOUNDS

I consider writing to be pen and paper therapy. I have 24-7 access, no appointment necessary, and insurance isn't required. I can scribble and edit without concern that I'm on a time limit or being evaluated by another person. When my pen and paper therapy session is over, I simply crumble and toss the paper away, not having to revisit the content unless I choose.

This week, I've had frequent encounters with pen and paper. Reading from Job 7 was particularly freeing. "I cannot keep from speaking. I must express my anguish. My bitter soul must complain...I would rather be strangled, rather die than suffer like this. (Job 7:11, 15 NLT). I always find there is a fine line between being open and honest with God and whining to God. I'm not despondent like Job was in this scripture, but I relate to his authenticity and extreme comfort in talking to his Creator. I'm most frustrated because gritty situations are showing up in different ways, but it's my rebellious pattern needing to be broken. Knowing without doing adds salt to a fresh water pond in the FROG blog.

Job experienced growth in his relationship with God because he was willing to expose his immense pain. I've seen a certain camaraderie occur when someone exposes a bullet wound to the heart (or body in some cases). As I wrote my "Dear God" letter, I had a stirring about what Jesus would be writing if He used pen and paper therapy for His war wounds.

When Jesus was in human form on earth, did He grow weary when people only approached Him when they needed healing or a meal? Did people ask Jesus how His day was going or how He felt? Did He eat leftovers, so others could indulge in second helpings of fish and bread? There is only one time in scripture when I read that Jesus cried His request to accomplish God's will by any other method than death by crucifixion.

What if Jesus and I were sitting around a campfire today comparing war wounds? Anything I've ever endured in nearly five decades will always pale to what He experienced in His earthly journey, yet He patiently and empathetically listens. I'm grateful that even though Jesus's pain supersedes anything I'll ever face, there is a closeness I've developed by sharing my battle scars and victories with Him.

My pen and paper therapy letters invite deeper healing through Jesus' faithful guardianship. Instead of denying or stuffing hardships I face on this side of heaven, I'm grateful that Jesus is only one call away. He welcomes walk-ins (or write-ins)!

Leaping out as a rescued prisoner of war in His freedom, Christina

AN UNLIKELY PRESCRIPTION

As I replay the ripples of conversation from my day, I'm nourished by an atypical solution from a friend's doctor. Susan (name changed) met with her physician to discuss fears that manifested from a series of isolated but distressing events. Her doctor shares Susan's faith beliefs and said he'd write an anti-anxiety prescription, but also handed her a bible with a #91 on the cover and pages marked with orange sticky tabs.

The #91 on the cover indicated how many bibles he had "prescribed" for his patients struggling with anxiety. He marked each scripture reference that teaches about inner turmoil. He invited Susan to take one orange "tab" as often as needed and allow the message to continually drip like a spiritual IV. She took the doctor's prescription for medicine as a back-up solution but said she's first going to use the Original Physician's instruction.

Peacefully enjoying the calm waters from the lily pad as I reflect on this holistic health approach, Christina

MORE THAN 24-HOUR PROTECTION

In the middle of worldly torrential happenings, I have a wave of thankfulness for God's protection over my corner of earth. Oak Ridge, TN has been spared of many natural (and unnatural) events. Our son works contract jobs for UXO and has been especially sheltered.

Todd (son) and his wife live in Kentucky and his job requires him to work everywhere but Kentucky. In a widespread area around his home, jobs are neither lucrative nor abundant. His job shelters his family from poverty, but extensive travel is required. He was hired to work in California earlier this year. Shortly after that job finished, California's soil was ravaged by wildfires.

His next assignment took him to Puerto Rico. Two weeks into that job, he was called out because Hurricane Maria's threats in Texas moved toward Puerto Rico. Initially, Todd and his co-workers scoffed at their job release because they said that section of Puerto Rico was never impacted with hurricanes. They originally defined these alerts as "over-rated." Todd was disappointed to leave because he loved Puerto Rico, his work team, and the overall work. Shortly after he was flown home to Kentucky, Hurricane Maria lashed with a vengeance.

He got stationed in Wisconsin, only minutes from family who did not settle in Tennessee and Kentucky. Wisconsin is where my Mom, Todd's granny, moved to heaven in 2015. He stayed away from the area that holds cherished memories with Granny. His job initiated him into reminiscing those years with an updated outlook.

I greet this morning with sunrise above my lily pad. God has protected Todd from poverty, wildfires, and a hurricane. He used a

86

job site to expose grief that required tedious heart excavation. The storms of life can be shifting winds that invite clean-up and restoration. God has spared our only son from devastation as He did with Jesus, His only Son. Darkness will not hold back His light because God has the final say!

With an ironic twist of appreciation. FROG-ing from a sheltered lily pad, Christina

AMISH FRIENDSHIP BREAD

My husband's Grandma Ziegler lived to be 99 years old and was
healthy up until her final weeks on earth. She was well-known for
her bakery treats and breads. Through her baking, she gave us a
taste of what "on earth as it is in heaven" means.

As Grandma Z aged, she relied on others to give her car rides. She
paid drivers in loaves of Amish Friendship Bread, which requires
ten days of preparation before the bread reaches the oven. Those
ten days are delayed gratification for anyone who has gotten to
savor her delicious recipe. If Friendship Bread was the manna
rained down from heaven, I don't know why the Israelites
complained during their 40-year desert journey!

Grandma taught us, via this bread's recipe, to respect the
development of life. Each of the ten-day steps requires action.
Some days, the recipe simply states to do nothing. Other days, it
instructs the baker to mash the plastic bag of ingredients. Other
days there are ingredients to add. In our modern-day methods of
quick breads and bread machines, some people steer from the
Amish Friendship Bread due to its extended process.

I see my life journey in that mixing bowl. I wish I had an actual
recipe to follow which told me what ingredients to add and in
which order. Or a recipe that offered suggestions for when the
batter of life gets too thick. Some days I'm called to be still. Some
days I experience an inner mashing. Sometimes I need to add
ingredients (like patience and gentleness). My prayers want a quick
bread version and I recognize that sometimes I disrespect the
measurement guidelines. In Grandma Z's glimpse-of-the century
mark, I'm sure she experienced many transitional steps. She
learned to patiently trust the processes. Grandma anticipated

results and accepted that each day was a building ingredient to complete her recipe card of life.

Instead of being satisfied with quick, often dry crumbly bread, I challenge myself to make friends with the pace of my Creator's process. I believe I'll bake more peace into the bread of life if I remove my stop watch and concentrate on God's grandfather clock.

Stirring up friendship bread recipes for life, Christina

IT'S ALL ABOUT WINNING

In a culture where trophies matter and everyone deserves an accolade, that tongue-in-cheek reference, "it's all about winning," rings true in many arenas. I see superlative headlines that include the best, favorite, biggest, and most. What if we strived to be the first to greet another person? The quickest to say thank you? The winner of giving the most smiles? The person who listens best?

I learned that a second grader in our school community was just diagnosed with leukemia. Gratefully, there have been many people to be "the firsts" to volunteer support. They have stepped up to the plate to take a swing at coordinating meals, transportation, gift cards, and visits.

What would my days look like if I responded to others' needs as promptly as these caring individuals did for our newly diagnosed friend? What would happen if I bridged gaps with intensity? How would my life be different if I became a more lavish giver? We hear countless stories about heroes during crisis. We watch unlikely people rising to be part of a solution amidst emergencies. Why do I sometimes stay in the woodwork until a problem arises? Could I avert potential heartache if I consistently offered encouragement instead of waiting until I could *see* that someone was lonely or lacking guidance?

Thank you to those people who have mailed me a card just because. I appreciate the leaders who first smiled at me in the grocery store or traffic jams. I'm grateful to those who have prioritized my prayers over their own challenges. I am humbled by those who have initiated affirmations when I could be categorized as least likely to deserve their light.

Lord, help me be a person who continually strives to look through the windows of someone's gaze. To be the first to open the blinds to brighten someone's view. To win the trust, uplift, and softening of someone's heart. Instead of waiting for an emergency or crisis, use me to provide encouragement as preventative maintenance against hopelessness. Everyone needs a trophy of uplifting team spirit.

To live a life where my Creator's approval is my greatest trophy,
Christina

A DOUBLE DARE

God's always up to something. Yesterday I wrote about being first, most, best, and favorite. Today I received a double dare as I listened to Pastor Rick Warren on a radio broadcast. He taught that the two most dangerous words to pray are, "use me."

Pastor Warren explained how someone who asks God to use them will never be bored. I thought of the game *Truth, Dare, Double Dare* we played as teenagers. A player was asked to tell the truth about any question that the questioner asked. A dare meant the player was challenged to complete a 'mildly scary activity.' A double dare tested the player's courageous meter to fulfill the pursuit. I witnessed double dares resulting in either false audacity to carry out the mission or prudence to know the risk may produce unpleasant consequences.

In my circle of friends, dare was often our prevailing choice. I wasn't willing to be vulnerable enough to place one of my lungs on a virtual chopping block by choosing the truth option. I also wasn't inclined to represent hypocrisy by making others wonder if my answer was the whole truth. Most of my friends weren't bold enough to choose a double dare, maybe out of wisdom or more likely from outright fear. A dare seemed to be the game's middle ground.

Use me. Truth, Dare, or Double Dare? As I near 50, exposing my truths, within reasonable limits, isn't as scary as it was when I was a teenager. I miss, or selectively "miss" God's first call (and the second, third...) but I'm usually cooperative if God calls me to use my *natural* talents. I'm sometimes willing to slightly stretch my schedule (aka "a dare"). A full-blown submission to use me with unconditional follow-through on His request? Now *that's* a double dare!

Growing in courage to align with my Creator's plans! I'm on His payroll. Help me accept double dare challenges and allow Him to use me, Christina

A LIGHT SANDWICH

My husband is conscientious about car maintenance and has a tremendous sense of vehicle precautions. He arranged to have new tires put on my car before my sister and I left for our annual trip to a mountain cabin. While the tires were being replaced I drove our older car that has been nudged along, but still runs. Ordinarily, I appreciate our elderly vehicle as a backup, but in this morning's pouring rain, I wished we had traded it in years ago.

My night vision resembles a raccoon's day vision. (Warning! Tangent sentence ahead. After my editor questioned how people determine things such as animal vision and who experiments on such things, I found an answer for his inquiring mind. Thanks to a trusted Google search: "Raccoons have excellent night vision. The reflective layer in the lens of the eye that makes raccoon eyes seem to glow red in the dark also magnifies images of nearby objects.") With that explanation to satisfy said editor's request, I remain under my 500 word FROG blog limit and hope I have not lost the reader's train of thought.

Please return from my visionary tangent without judging the lack of transition sentence. The rain and shiny road glare heightened my coordination of finding wipers, lights, defrost, and heat switches. I drove ten miles under the speed limit and asked God to light my path and protect me. Less than a mile later, there was a large truck whose driver paced my trek slightly faster than I drove. I looked in my rearview mirror and saw a shorter vehicle traveling behind me, perfectly lighting the curves that made the road brighter. It was like God reminding me that He goes before me *and* stands behind me. He sandwiched me between two moving metal hedges of protection. God used both headlights and tail lights to light the road for each other.

Despite the rainy morning darkness, our vehicle lights beamed on the path for one another. Some were leading lights, some were supportive background lights, but all helped guide others toward their destination.

Help me align with other lights. Help me shed light on others as we leap from lily pad to lily pad, Christina

FREE SPIRITED DEPENDENCY

Sunrises above the Tennessee lily pad have been intensely dynamic this fall. Vibrant reds, bubble gum pinks, silvery lilacs, and gleaming yellows resemble the shades Thomas Kinkade painted. The growing morning light produces significant cotton balls in the sky, inviting cloud watchers to relish horizon images. On mornings like this, I'd rather have my head in those clouds than on my paved commute.

I drove to work and stole as many glances upward as safely possible. There were four black birds flying in one direction until the flock's wing man changed direction. I looked up again and almost out of nowhere a separate flock of about 60 birds flew, but they didn't join the other four black birds. It looked like a feathered display of fireworks! I smiled out loud because I thought about their free flying spirit. Those birds have physical freedom. As a believer and follower of Jesus, I have spiritual freedom.

That freedom generates from trusting in His promises. I know my Creator has a plan for my life. I am to cast my cares on Him and trust His ways are much wiser than mine. It's when I doubt God's promises that I lose my freedom. When I live according to my agenda, my independence can cause anxiety, self-reliability, and hasty decisions. My free spirit can turn a bird's flight into bird droppings!

Jesus bought me with *all* His blood. The Bible said that when the soldier pierced Jesus' side only water trickled from His body. He gave everything. He gave up His freedom from sin to undergo an earthly journey. Even though Jesus left heaven to join the human experience, He was never independent of His Father. If I represent

Jesus, I must release my independence. I am to be free *with* Him, not free *from* Him.

Birds experience amazing views as they rise above concrete to see the tops of mountains. They have a level of personal freedom, yet are solely dependent on many atmospheric factors. Their birdie knees naturally bow just as my knees unnaturally bend in surrender to a Higher Power. Free, but in-dependence of Him.

I want to be more soul-ly dependent on my Creator. With my head in the clouds, Christina

MOUTHWASH AND SAUERKRAUT SAVE THE DAY

Sauerkraut and mouthwash are typically not considered to combat mental battles. I discovered these hidden gems are highly effective when I struggle with anxiety or recognize the need to delay words (i.e. bite my tongue).

When I encountered acute grief, I stumbled into paralyzing anxiety. I was in a valley too deep to seek counselors. Any decision beyond which socks to wear caused substantial panic. I mostly practice most natural remedies for holistic health and read how kefir, sauerkraut, yogurt, and berries rated highest on a list for decreasing edginess.

Dairy was not a digestive option and berries were not in season during these unpredictable anxiety breakouts. Two tablespoons of sauerkraut became one of my breakfast choices to combat nervousness. (Depending on differences in taste buds and food preferences, eating sauerkraut may trigger anxiety. Dave Dutrow, who wishes to remain anonymous, attests to this statement)! Sauerkraut's vinegar had bite, but the benefits of pickled cabbage made the initial sting worthwhile. I've been gratefully delivered from explosive panic symptoms and appreciate the gift of sauerkraut when I needed it.

The other preventative remedy I incorporate is mouthwash. Mornings get a bit intense as my husband and I leave for work simultaneously. I sometimes snip at Tig because I want to finish one more thing and somehow the minutes before we launch out the door shift into high-speed. Other days, when I've had tremendous ideas evolving from morning quiet time I begin abundantly telling Tig as much as possible during those last crucial minutes. We both leave the house with our heads spinning because I started topics too detailed to cover in 180 seconds. Enter mouthwash.

I resist urges to verbally flood the air waves by grabbing mouthwash when I put the final touches into getting out the door on time. I use a mouthwash brand that requires 60-90 seconds of swishing so that means my lips stay closed from potential snipping *or* power talking. I'm able to focus on what to pack for the day because I'm not engaging my mouth in talking (unless I want to wipe minty fresh mouthwash from the floor or front of my clothes). It's refreshing to find remedies from unlikely sources.

A double dose of leaping healthily from the lily pad, Christina

LEAP FROG LIVING

My husband and I chose Amy Grant's *"I Need a Silent Night"* as our theme song to prepare for Christmas this year. We laid claim to inner peace, *living* stillness instead of merely reading about quieting the spirit. Each evening, Tig and I sit in front of candles inviting intentional calmness. We write prayers and praises in a journal so on New Year's Day we can reflect upon changes we will experience during this seasonal quest for peace.

Initially, I gratefully accepted a gentler presence. As December progressed, my calendar of events seemed to crowd restful awareness. My thoughts began to accelerate, and I started mentally living ahead of schedule. The days leading to December 25th included my Daddy's extended visit, a theatre role in a Christmas production, treats to bake, final exams at school, and gatherings with our granddaughters.

Tig and I practice minimalist living and forego retail hype. Our home remains simply decorated and we adhere to a three-gift exchange to represent gold, frankincense and myrrh. We delay Christmas party invitations until January and February when winter magically increases our free time. Despite the simplicity of our season strategies, my spirit refused to adhere to the gentle atmosphere we crafted.

I engaged in a mental game of leap frog in December. I semi-focused on the present but immediate pressures seemed too intense so I mentally jumped onto the back of the next activity. It's as if my (false) logic believed it could pre-live the moment, that somehow if I mentally jumped past an event, I'd arrive sooner? Writing and editing that logic sounds silly but it's my reality. The daunting reality is I began mentally leap frogging all December activities, whether it was positively anticipated or "otherwise."

Instead of "simply" accepting and enjoying an unfolding process of life, I find myself speeding through days as if getting to the finish line for the sake of ending *is* the goal. Again, my lack of thought restraint leaves me overwhelmed and disappointed. In a season of fullness, I emptily hurry to the next thing. Spoiler alert Christina. There will always be a next thing. Reality check Christina. No matter what that thing may be, there will always be another thing.

My quest for increased stillness, no matter what season, must be frequently claimed. Mental stillness leads me to peace. Like someone newly learning the alphabet, a person fully concentrates on each letter. I'm going back to my early childhood days by reciting first A, *then* B, *then* C, *then*…. Instead of speed singing through that catchy little diddy, I slow the pace to honor and value each letter. Today's lesson in the lily pad is brought to me via leap frog and the alphabet song.

Slowing from a leap frog to a creep frog pace, processing one letter at a time, Christina

A DOUBLE LESSON

I'm chuckling as I write this. I received a nearly instantaneous lesson from yesterday's leap frog reflection. I discussed mentally jumping ahead of time with disregard for the present moment. Hours after I posted the blog, our six-year old granddaughter responded to a situation in a way her Grams has been living.

I picked up Marley Mae from her house and said that Grams had surprises, activities, and outings for our weekend visit. She wanted a detailed agenda and I assured her we would fully enjoy each idea as it happened. I invited her to embrace alternative plans that may later be revealed. We talked about being peaceful and train our eyes to be like a camera, ready to capture each piece of a picture as it presented itself.

She accepted this in-the-moment guideline during our first few outings and errands. As the day unfolded, she was ready for a break and possibly a nap. I didn't want to end our fun, so I took her for a spontaneous ice cream treat. As we waited in line for our order, I silently congratulated myself for refraining from leap frog living. I wanted our visit to remain more than an activity checklist. Marley Mae was honoring our staying-present-in-the-moment approach.

No sooner had my observation surfaced, Marley Mae asked, "Grams? What are we going to do after we have our ice cream?" We hadn't even gotten our ice cream and she was anticipating eating it, throwing away our dessert trash, and heading out the door to explore the future.

Prior to writing yesterday's FROG blog, I probably would have answered Marley Mae with the next hour's plans instead of guiding her to appreciate the experience that was right in front of us. Marley Mae and I are learning from each other. We're in training to understand presence together. I grasp how much simpler life is when I watch other people's lessons rather than practicing them myself.

Seeing my reflection through a six-year old leap frogging in the pond, Christina

EXPANSION PROJECT IN FORCE

With full expectation of a New Year, full anticipation of fresh dreams, full excitement of a long break between Christmas and January 1, I also carry a full belly. I'm grateful for abundant blessings of holiday treats and vacation time. That delightful abundance of fudge, trail mix, and peanut blossom cookies has resulted in clothes that have "shrunk." I have a functioning dryer with appropriate heat settings, so I need to face the truth about my "magically" shrinking clothes.

I've enjoyed the holiday relaxation and bounty and it's time to implement my technique for re-establishing more exercise. I feel best when I stay active at least an hour a day, exercising in two, sometimes three half-hour installments. During a previous career path, I hit a significant patch of minimal exercise due to job circumstances. I got back to healthier habits by incorporating a fifteen-minute challenge. I united purpose with a plan to incorporate an hour of walking daily, done in four fifteen-minute increments.

The first fifteen-minute installment is the simplest for me because I love greeting the-morning and clearing my head by walking shortly after waking. The second fifteen-minute block is to exercise our dogs before I head out for the day. The third fifteen-minute set is for Vitamin D via outdoor light, fresh air, and mid-day check-up for my spirit. Sometimes the lunch block includes a walk-and-talk life coaching session, so I get a mind uplifting bonus. I walk with my husband for the fourth fifteen-minute segment. Depending on how our days are spent and what conversations surface, our spouse walk often extends beyond a quarter of an hour.

Those sixty minutes of daily movement remain the same no matter how they're allotted, but I'm most motivated when I match a mission with each exercise installment. One for me, one for the dogs, one for self/clients, one for my husband. This balance has helped me build relationships and a stronger core with relative simplicity. The short frequent walks have been like a spiritual equivalent to praying without ceasing. They expand my positive focus instead of expanding my waistline!

With widespread motivation toward healthy habits, Christina

A KITCHEN AIDE

I recently completed my eleven-year work-in-progress, *Life's Too Short for Dull Razors, Cheap Pens, and Worn-Out Underwear.* It was time to stop dating my book dream and commit to a relationship that began a decade ago between pen and yellow lined legal pad.

I've cast my lines in other waters and when I evaluated my progress from this year's personal growth plan, I am going to fire up a powerboat but intentionally sail at a row boat pace. While I FROG (Fully Rely On God) along on my lily pad, I'm inviting new meaning to the worldly hype to "be more." Some new definitions of "be more in life" resemble a back float instead of my typical dog paddle. I will be more compassionate (be less harsh). I will be more reflective (be less of a glaring light). I will be more aware of my responses (be less reactive).

Several authors have written about the value of presence over perfection. I've benefitted from their insight, especially one morning after my alarm went off. Immediately I began calculating the next 16 hours of my day and could almost hear Jesus when He interrupted Martha's litany. Martha was cooking, cleaning the house, preparing for guests, dotting i's and crossing t's. The more she ticked off her list, the more she got ticked off at her sister Mary who was listening to Jesus teach. In Martha's defense, I believe many hands make light work. I wonder how the story would have altered if Mary had been more helpful, been more alert, been more aware of what Martha was doing. Maybe they both would have gotten the benefit of Jesus' teaching!

With conflict brewing hotter than the stove, Jesus stepped in to extinguish Martha's fire. He figuratively wiped the ashes from Martha's face and fixed her squeaky oven hinges (aka her mouth). Jesus explained that meal preparation can wait, His teaching was now. Point taken to my present (over perfect) 16-hour day. Before I got out of bed already mentally drained to seize the upcoming day, I think Jesus said, "Martha, Martha, you worry about much. Listen more, talk less. Be more still. Be more gentle." Jesus gracefully changed Martha's story name to protect my identity.

The spirit tether guided me toward inventorying what was on my grocery list (growth plan). I was to focus on each seasoning, each measurement and blend accordingly. Instead of transforming my hours into a casserole or stir fry, I will be more with less. I can be more like comforting mashed potatoes. Few ingredients, many positive reviews. Help me not to waffle on my "be more" grill!

Gently dipping into the pond from the FROG blog, Christina

WRITTEN THERAPY

I needed to schedule a therapy session this morning. Fortunately, my pen and paper therapists answer house calls and are available 24-7. During a desert time of my life, writing was something I could do effectively. Pen and paper supplied relief from severe heartbreak. Those written therapy sessions allowed my thoughts to confidentially bleed out as I labored to move forward.

I've reclaimed emotional grounding since then, but today I temporarily relived that once familiar desperation. I fostered a cactus-like demeanor. A metaphorical camel pressed its' thudding hooves over my heart. I kick back this virtual desert sand by sharing a coping strategy I used during acute grief.

After my Mom moved to heaven in 2015, I expected fatigue. I understood random tears. I identified with a heavy spirit and angst during the tedious grieving process. However, I didn't fathom truckloads of anxiety to be dumped at my heart's doorstep. Indecisiveness isn't my natural default so when I found myself stressing about which vegetables to put on my salad, I panicked. Those gripping bouts of uncertainness became frequently intense.

I'd sit at my desk paralyzed by terror with nothing remotely dangerous to fear. Some unseen force compelled me to the chair and I was too afraid to move for no evident cause. I felt suffocated from unexplainable fright and spear and shield became protective weapons. I grabbed paper and pen like life preservers. I wrote tidal waves of swirling thoughts as fast as I could. I feverishly scribbled everything that unnerved me, without concern that someone may discover this chaotic battle and judge me. I wrote quickly, daring my hand to match the pace of my heart. When I released my pen from its scripted marathon, I was sweating from release of soul toxins.

For weeks during acute grief, pen and paper therapy worked effectively. As I regained strength during this unsettling period, I used less paper because I grew tired of writing similar expressions masked behind different faces. I discovered thought patterns through writing and realized I was overdue to get past my polluted assessments.

To invite forward motion thinking, I started copying pages from a motivational quote book. The higher my tension pulsed, the more quickly I scrawled inspirational excerpts. I noticed as I penned uplifting quotes, my spirit followed its elevated lead. I began flagging pages of enriching books so when distress came knocking, I opened the door to handwrite positive messages.

I used this "write the light" solution to unstick my toxic trap. When I confronted a battle of nerves, I fought by copying optimistically energizing books. Sometimes time constraints allowed only a few written sentences instead of an entire page. Sometimes anxiety presented itself at "geographically inconvenient moments", (font: tongue-in-cheek) so I visualized writing previous encouragements to invite calmness to return. Simply the image of writing moved me beyond negative tension and quieted mental scatter. This history lesson became my future blessin'.

Leaping worry free (for this moment) from the lily pad, Christina

A SAILING VESSEL

I'm on an assignment that involves a 40-minute commute. To someone in Los Angeles, a 40-minute commute is miniscule. To someone in rural Kentucky, that is the average drive time to get to Wal-Mart or a convenience store. To the person sitting in this chair, the commute is significant because I used to have the luxury of working five minutes from home.

This commute is weighty because it requires me to significantly surrender my career timeline for God's job alignment. I'm driving to complete a mission for what I consider a Nineveh experience. I know I've been called to this project, but it's been a whale of a time.

Ironically the longer commute has transpired into the best part of this assignment. I listen to music, podcasts, witness amazing sunrises and sunsets. I've drafted many initially random thoughts into published articles, future books, and stand-up comedy routines. I pull out of our neighborhood to drive to the job site and humor myself by saying, "It's time to collect future writing material."

I remain accident free (and ticket free) through countless traveling mercies. I've talked to God about things I didn't even know existed in me to discuss. I have sought His advice, clarity, and prayed for people I haven't thought about in years. I see a fellow traveler who resembles someone from a past interaction and pray for the "look alike" and the recollected person. I pass a car that reminds me of a person who drives a similar vehicle and use the recall to pray for both drivers. My Nissan Juke wheels have spiritually taken me to places that travel beyond any highway.

To honor this Nineveh assignment, I nicknamed my Juke, Jonah. If I had a bumper sticker for Jonah, it would read, "This car is a prayer mobile." Jonah has kept me afloat beyond the belly of a whale!

Lessons and blessins, Christina

P.S. I wonder if prior to Nineveh, Jonah was an avid whale watcher? ☺

A SINGLE OR A DOUBLE?

I was drafting an article query for a magazine that has previously published my work. An odd fear knocked on the leaves of my lily pad in the FROG blog. Cockroach-like thoughts crept from hiding places in my mind. I've learned to flick on lights to make many creepy feelings scurry. Often, I speak out whatever half-truth or lie is coming out of my inner darkness. I needed to expose the source of these creepy-crawly judgments.

I grabbed my journal and wrote a brain dump of concerns about sending the magazine query. 'What if the editor thinks I'm nagging to send a block of articles all at once?' 'How do I write a follow-up to a magazine that has purchased previous work?' 'This story is already a hot topic and based on my trip to Books-A-Million yesterday, my idea is trendier than I anticipated.' 'Why should I add more written voice to an overpopulated platform?'

Mid-sentence of trapping the wings of another cockroach thought, I reread the apprehensions I had written. The punctuation stood out. I had used single quotation marks around each worry woe. Those single bookends marked paraphrasing. Journalism 101 taught me that an author uses double quotation marks only when she uses a subject's exact citation. My mind breaking news story was grossly paraphrased with a jaded slant. Those single ticks hovered around unfounded fears and it was time to edit my original mental script.

After each paraphrased concern, I used double quotation marks for a rewritten perspective:

'What if the editor thinks I'm nagging to send a block of articles all at once?'
"The editor may appreciate multiple selections to publish. The editor may use all or none of the material. Query anyway."

'How do I write a query to offer more magazine material after they already bought previous work?' "Christina? There's this new thing that began in 1998 called a Google search? You're not the first person to write multiple articles for numerous magazines. Google is your friend."

'This story is already a hot topic and based on my trip to Books-A-Million yesterday, my idea is trendier than I anticipated.' "What if auto makers left their chassis ideas on their work benches after driving Henry Ford's Model T? Keep your wheels turning to offer your own spin on the subject.

'Why should I add written voice to an overpopulated platform?' "What if architects stopped creating house plans because there are already vast amounts of blueprints?"

When viewing my writing profession through the lens of less murky waters, I replace single quotation paraphrases with authentic statements. Marked by double doses of faith instead of single-minded fears.

With a brighter look from the lily pad, Christina

HONESTLY?

"To be honest with you, I think that…" "Honestly, if this keeps going on…" "Honestly? That doesn't surprise me." These are word threads that frequently weaved patterns into conversations this week. I've heard an increase in people interjecting the word "honestly" in dialogue or prefacing a statement with "to be honest with you." Unlike filler words such as um, uh, and er, I wonder why honesty is quantified.

A friend shared a funny story about her son. Parts of her recap included, "Honestly? I forget that she would…"and "To be honest with you, I wonder if…" We have a close relationship so after she finished, it was in a lighthearted tone that I asked her to verify her honesty. She answered with a laughed, "Honestly? I don't know why I say 'to be honest with you' because I *am* an honest person! It's just something I picked up in listening to other people talk." We joked about possible reactions if we interrupted someone who used honestly in their description. We wondered how people would answer if we asked for the dishonest version of their conversation.

The FROG blog isn't designed to preach from a lily pad, so I plunge into the pond with simple (honest) questions. Am I being honest (and kind) with my words? Honesty and kindness is not always the same thing. I often struggle with one over the other in some situations. Am I speaking truth or merely spouting my opinion? Are there areas in my life where my viewpoint is *not* completely honest? What places do I need to keep quiet because honesty isn't the best approach?

Looking deep in the reflective pond as I ask all honesty to surface,
Christina

THROWING DIRT

A friend works for a search and rescue squad and is training her dog to become her professional partner. Mateo is a golden retriever pup with an assertive personality and energy bubbling from every fiber of his furry body. He is slow to wear out and quick to rejuvenate so he requires heavy amounts of exercise before any training can take place.

Juli built a sandbox for Mateo so he can dig and hunt for various objects she hides in the sand. On the first day the sandbox was introduced, Mateo dug three solid hours with very short breaks. When he was panting, lying down, and nearly falling asleep with his head up, Joni finally gained his attention long enough to teach commands.

She tells animated stories about creatively depleting Mateo's extra vigor while simultaneously training him. These antics have been entertaining until I recognized how much Mateo and I have in common. I'm starting a new phase of my business and many puzzle pieces are aligning, but larger pieces remain in a pregnant pause.

I have spent countless hours knocking on doors, opening windows of ideas, developing partnerships, and mentally arranging possibilities. The digging is motion within what appears to be an endless sandbox. I know there are treasures to be found yet unburying them is like excavating quicksand.

With dirt flying every which way in my mind, I realize that like Juli, my Creator allows me to plow, burrow, and tunnel life's sandpits. He's gently observing and protecting me from heat exhaustion, but patiently waits until I finally wear out. He only knows when I have hollowed out a pit wide enough to collect pools of my own sweat will He have my attention. For now, I realize He's waiting for me to drain my excessive energy before He can effectively train me to meet His assignments. By walking outside or writing unedited streams of consciousness, I can accelerate the adrenaline dump so I am more ready for His teaching. Maybe Mateo would allow me to dig next to him in his sandpit!

With greater understanding of this K-9 version of obedience school, I'm commanding myself to rest my lily pad on a sand dune.

From a toadstool in the FROG blog, Christina

FILL 'ER UP!

A goal from this year's growth plan includes reviewing my 2015-2017 journals. Those three years are framed around what I label "The Desert Years." After face-planting into large dunes, I finally began replacing the sandy grit with pearls of wisdom. The original entries appeared as an agonizing mirage in the arid ground of my soul. In hindsight, these optical illusions became beacons for future insight.

From an April 12, 2016 entry: "I know I should be faithful in small every-day things. If I want to be promoted to larger projects or greater ministry, I must focus on training my character. My mind is full, my spirit is empty. I'm in a grueling spiritual workout. Just *watching* this fitness video isn't going to build any forward moving muscle. My internal core has grown flabby. It's even more painful to recognize I'm waiting for someone else to run this leg of my race while I sit back and expect to reap fitness benefits. I'm in a spiritual dark hole, but my head is clattering with noise. I need Your clear direction!"

Writing those words was like lifting dead curls from the floor of my heart. Surprisingly, reading those words with a different "tone" now reveals a stronger mind, soul, and body development. Through that written pain I see results from that virtuous marathon. I write this to remind myself to regularly monitor the steps of my spiritual pedometer. I also need to realize what measuring tool I am using. Physical progress is sometimes more evident by monitoring the scale or tape measure. I've found that my spiritual progress can be monitored by an increased peace as I frequent God's presence and track with His pace.

I am to walk my earthly mission on a forward moving treadmill and not use my faith fitness equipment as a clothes rack.

Daily walking at least 10,000 steps with my Creator, Christina

BOUGHT "AS IS"

My husband and I are in the market for a newer vehicle. Tig's truck has 280,000 miles on its nearly 20-year chassis. Our recent evening walks lead to neighborhood dealership lots. Our country drives are to inspect vehicles for sale.

Some of our finds are sold "as is." Some cars have limited warranties while others have bumper-to-bumper guarantees. Each option is reflected in the asking price. The more extensive warranty guarantees the buyer a proportionally extensive cost. Whatever we purchase will assuredly depreciate after we drive off the lot.

I present an "As Is" Model C (for Christina) on the world's auction block. On my journey, I sometimes run into (virtual) walls, gun my motor (mouth), hit roadblocks, and burden my transmission by excessively shifting gears (changing my directional mind). The difference between my life and a car's life is when I pass from earth's parking lot, I have an eternal lifetime warranty bought 2000 years ago with the most inflated price.

Gratefully, Jesus didn't shy away from sticker shock. He went to the intersection of the cross and stopped traffic, so I could freely pass. When I accepted Him as my soul provider, He unconditionally agreed to handle all road hazards on my trek. He is my bumper-to-bumper, unlimited mileage coverage even when my headlights grow dim and I fishtail into life's barricades. He bought me "as is" but offered His eternal life guarantee. However, I still must take advantage of His warranty, which covers certain things, but I must remember to actually use it. The explanation of my warranty is written in 1 Cor. 15:20-30 and 2 Tim 2:3-13.

In thanksgiving for lifetime warranties signed and sealed in His Blood, Christina

GENTLE TENACITY

Gentle tenacity. That combination originated from someone asking me to describe a friend's unique characteristics in two words. When I first grouped those terms, gentle and tenacity sounded like antonyms. Lucy (name changed) is soft-spoken. Her conversational word count is low, yet she carries fierce passion. I consider her a modern-day female John Wayne. She faces regular anxiety attacks but saddles up anyway to ride through her inner storms.

Lucy doesn't allow her petite stature or quiet nature to keep her from serving on a Search and Rescue squad. She's intensely fearful of heights but is working toward fire department certification. Lucy knows carrying a 45- pound pack while climbing 35-45 feet on a free-standing ladder is part of her screening process. She's motivated by a greater cause to save lives. She fights her potential frustration with humble determination. Even in gritty situations, Lucy is like a loofah that cleans without being abrasive.

Jesus' mother Mary lived with gentle tenacity. Thirteen-year old Mary said yes to an angel's message that she would bear the Savior of the world, before asking for her parents' approval. She watched pre-teen Jesus teach church elders in the synagogue. Mary didn't turn into Mama Bear or Helicopter Mom as she watched Jesus carry His cross up Calvary. She silently but courageously suffered. She knew her role and accepted what she was called to do. She knew she was to be peacefully steadfast amid extreme circumstances, even when she most likely struggled with human doubt.

Gentle tenacity reminds me of how opposites can attract and harmoniously grow. I want to have a meekness sewn together with durable, reinforced seams.

Seeking quiet and strength from an anchored lily pad, Christina

PIER PRESSURE

A water-logged reflection from the lily pad. I walked a marina trail and observed early morning fishermen. Some fishermen casted from a boat, some fished from the lake bank, and some threw their lines from the pier. All fishermen appeared to have a similar quest, to reel in a catch. I was curious to know their beneath-the-surface stories that brought them to the lake. Did they show up at the water's edge with their spirit resembling net fishing or spear fishing? Spear fishing and net fishing both spawn a catch, but the procedure is drastically distinctive.

Figuratively, we're in a similar boat on earth. We navigate various water sources, practice diversity in sailing our life vessels, and use assorted bait, yet we dive into common hunting zones. We're fishing for why and how our life stream flows into a larger ocean. Sometimes we "flounder." Hopefully, we're searching within awake zone instead of a no wake zone! Am I using the right bait? If I fish using the wrong lure, the chances of reeling in what I'm trying to catch will go down hook, line, and sinker.

I waver between wanting to jump from my boat with carefree abandon and hunkering near the hull. I naturally dance many rapids, but sometimes rationalize that I'm 'waiting out a storm' (i.e. avoidance or delaying a decision). Occasionally, I'm guided to seek protection from verifiable hazard, not because of some concocted danger I imagined.

I write the FROG blog to represent Fully Rely On God. There's a continual paddle to *live* what I write, and to faithfully *practice* what I learn and understand. To some extent, people of all ages globally experience a burden of comparison and peer pressure. As an adult, I face an altered description of 'pier pressure.'

If I *say* God is my Captain who is responsible for all water to sail my course, why do I cling to worldly piers for protection (i.e. money, creature comforts, completed checklists)? Other times, I use a pier to jump into water which isn't mine to swim. I use my piers (prayer times) to load and unload concerns and joys onto my Creator's barge.

I was conditioned from childhood to trust manmade planks and I need faith to bank on God's board of truth. I'm growing to expect God's immovable anchor for all refuge. In the sometimes-tumultuous water of my inner vessel, when I use the Creator's Pier as my command station, I can enjoy carefree dock jumping into any water He chooses.

Jesus, continue navigating my course so I may wisely channel 'pier pressure.' Help me be a fisher of men by using a net, not a spear. Help me understand that sometimes it's necessary to confront someone with a "spear" to keep them out of harm's way but help me be more like Jesus who used compassion when He confronted truth.

Be my Lifeguard, Christina

THE POWER WORD DIFFERENCE

I'm training myself to develop a gentler tone of living. While searching for resources to guide me toward a less rigid approach, I discovered Eckart Tolle's teachings. https://www.eckharttolle.com/

Tolle features philosophies about stream of consciousness, non-judgmentally accepting whatever a situation presents, beyond immediate safety concerns. He discusses how living minute to minute often diffuses much volatile energy and inner conflict.

I'm incorporating two summary words to practice Tolle's invitation to be mindfully accessible. Instead of labeling encounters as good and/or bad, I use an uplifting word when an interaction coincides with my original expectation. For example: a meal. Prior to this vocabulary makeover, I may have described the meal with many yummy adjectives, all according to me. However, if the dish included tomatoes or pickles, my husband would describe the meal as anything but delicious, according to him. He's not wrong, I'm not right. I'm not good. He's not bad. We have differing opinions. This freestyle flow greets the next instant with anticipation to discover fresh descriptions of the moment.

Another example: A phone call. I'm training myself to simply observe the call with suspended judgment. If the conversation ended well, according to me, if I need to comment, I summarize with "spectacular" or perhaps "fulfilling." If the phone call included strained dialogue, according to me, I respond in a contemplative tone, "Hmmm. Different." When I don't categorize or dissect situations as I had been, gentler tone manifests.

An interruption from karma, irony, or perhaps a message from the electronic universe. During the last edit of this writing, I received "an unexpected opportunity to practice" what it means to embrace the moment with gentleness. What you are reading is a modification from my original message. "Hmmm. Different." I neared the final publishing version when the power flickered. I chuckled at the lights flashing because the timing appeared to be an immediate internship for the gentle living lesson I just wrote.

The power recovered after a one second surge. I continued editing. The next surge lasted long enough to darken our neighborhood. As I gingerly stumbled to grab a flashlight, I jokingly said, "Hmmm. Different."

Time passed with no power and I noted how my utopia perception about Amish communities 'living simpler' is a better imagined fallacy than actuality, according to me. My present moment reality of that non-fictional black out was, "Hmmm. Different". Power was restored after an hour and when I rebooted the computer, reset each alarm and adjusted timers, I could only say, "Hmmm. Different" (in a less optimistically contemplative tone).

I want my in-the-moment adjectives to be associated with power words such as thoughtful, compassionate, and pleasant.

From a reference point which is sometimes different than expected, I light up the lily pad in the FROG blog at the present minute, Christina

ANTICIPATION VS EXPECTATION

During car racing season, Tig uses non-scheduled time to participate in various "gearhead events." Sometimes we go to car shows, truck pulls, demolition derbies, and mud bogs together, but often I prefer he independently connect with other guys and auto enthusiasts. I use his guy time to hike, try new cafes, crochet, visit book stores, and listen to random music lists (i.e. spanning from smooth jazz to 70's country to Broadway tunes).

When Tig and I dated, I wasn't as aware of our time apart because I focused on our next phone call or outing. I anticipated more and expected less before we were married. I was satisfied with less time because I knew we'd greet each other with enthusiasm, offer small but frequent gifts, and exchange handwritten notes. We genuinely listened, hanging on to whatever the other person said as if it would be our last conversation.

My anticipation used to outweigh expectation. Much research and writing has been done about depleted romance and communication gaps in long-term relationships. Tig and I have a nearly 26-year marriage which has rarely represented a flat-terrain walk. On a 1-10 scale, with 10 being the pinnacle, we agree that our overall relationship maintains a 7-8 score. Most of our marital uphill climbs generate after falsely expecting a long coasting speed, somehow believing we can love at a neutral pace. We collide when we steer from initiating creative ways to gift the other spouse. When we limit or stop appreciating thoughtful gestures, we arrive at a stonewalling gridlock.

When I increase self-focused expectation, I decrease simple anticipation. I sometimes presume my husband can and will bridge life's gaps, resulting in a virtual marital demo derby, driving against each other. Score keeping stemming from my expectations erode the foundation of our initial carefree energy.

We heard a pastor preach about selfless love and he uniquely described a reason he believes people become irritated and distant. He said, "Our egos are always striving to be on top. We become annoyed with others only when someone clearly isn't as passionate about pursuing our personal greatness. We expect others to celebrate us how we want and promote us when we want."

Creator of love please increase my generous anticipation when I slip into patterns of self-centered expectation. With anticipated expectation of God's movement, Christina

SADDLING UP SLOWLY

"Talk low, talk slow, and don't talk much" -John Wayne

With a rise in organic food production and utilizing natural resources, I'm intrigued that our communication processes don't match this growing trend. I use a flip phone (yes, I'm writing and living this statement in 2018), check email and voice mail twice a day, and text only if it's one of the pre-programmed "insert quick text" messages in my phone.

I've watched so many people allow themselves to be controlled by their phones and computers. These devices are incredibly valuable and link us to opportunities that John Wayne didn't encounter when he saddled up for his day. I'm concerned that these networks have become technological umbilical cords, possibly cutting off life that needs to be naturally birthed.

We have a family mantra, "If nobody is hurt or killed, then the rest of life is simply inconvenient." Outside of emergencies, I've discovered that my slower response time often produces organic solutions. When I'm less wrinkled, options (nearly) seamlessly unfold. The original intensity of a situation may not require permanent press as the steam naturally releases the creases of life.

Some people in my circle question if I'm concerned about missing what may be coming down the pipeline. Creation wasn't designed to live in the future and I've become more intentional about trusting God to carry me one breath at a time. I can't postdate a breath or breathe ahead of time so like John Wayne's pointed style, I hoof it one step at a time. Others choose to gallop their race horses through life. I've come to prefer an ambling gait. Faster than a walk, but slower than a gallop.

With wholesome food for thought (ful) paces, Christina

GUIDELINE OR GODLINE?

In preparation for today's adventures, there was swirling water around the lily pad as my mind swam in every pond but the current one. Most of the time when my mind moves faster than my body, I'm able to ground myself by handwriting thoughts and prioritize accordingly. It's a process I call (tongue-in-cheek), "Time for my mind to meet my paper." I hadn't spent as much time stilling my heart during morning quiet time, resulting in my think tank becoming more of a shark tank.

When I'm suffering from analysis paralysis in deciding the day's order of tasks, I begin one simple job, such as emptying wastebaskets or the dishwasher. I gain momentum and direction by accomplishing a less significant task and gradually move toward more noteworthy quests (as defined by me).

As I sped through my morning agenda to avoid becoming trapped, I caught myself moving for the sake of motion. I was (nearly) obsessing to cross things off that paper just to mark things off. Had my guideline become a god? Was I idolizing works more than checking in with God's use of His payroll for the day?

I took a step back to review my accomplishments (again, as defined by me). I realized I had jumped ahead to play a game of follow the leader and appointed myself as leader. I believe certain people and projects were placed on my heart at the beginning of the day but instead of following the Leader, I assumed roles that weren't mine to play. I was playing a role rather than praying a role under God's leadership.

Creator, thank You for the assignments you place on my heart. Protect me from turning my checklist and works into a god. Guard me against judging between meaningful and seemingly meaningless tasks according to myself. Grant me wisdom to know if I am to play a role or pray a role in completing Your plans.

Your servant seeking Your role, Christina

ENGRAVED IN PENCIL

My calendar is full today. Significant reality check: any time I begin a new writing that indicates my time, my material possession, my idea, I've learned that reflects the nature of my spirit, consumed by the shadow of myself. Leaping out of my spotlight to complete today's FROG blog...

Just as a parent or teacher guides a child to stop crying long enough to articulate the source of their tears, I received a similar interruption from my Father. Prior to writing this blog, I was complimenting myself about how much I had on my agenda, yet I was growing toward creating larger margins between assignments. I wrote appointments and added a * next to time gaps as if that * was an adult version of a smiley face or gold star.

I've worked to balance the biblical Martha with Mary and when I reviewed my daily game plan, I sensed an inner tug. What if x, y, and z (or d, e, and f) were ahead of schedule, delayed, or didn't happen at all? Would I peacefully rewrite the day? Would I dismiss that assignment completely?

I closed my calendar, grabbed a blank piece of paper and pencil. The pencil was important because I primarily write with blue ink pens. I chose the pencil to represent a willingness to believe my Creator had ideas for my day if I'd ask (ya think?). It also had a new eraser to indicate a surrender to modify as He edited my calendar.

I said out loud, "Father, I use this blank paper and pencil to symbolize surrender to allow Your plans to supersede my agenda. I only know the present moment, but you see my entire day. Help me erase or add according to Your ink that designs my path. Draw

133

me into your blueprints and allow me to use the flow of Your pen to write each of the upcoming 1440 minutes of this day." Side note for sanity check: when I offered this prayer out loud, I was alone in my car and not in a public place!

Trusting my Creator to engineer and rebuild my day, Christina

SIGN OF THE TIMES

Our city department has made significant effort to simplify navigating our streets by implementing more signage. With the increased directional guidelines, I believe I've become more confused. We recently had two round-abouts installed near a busy shopping center. There are now colorful arrows, speed limit and merge signs, and crosswalk pictures for blocks before each round-about.

The new round-about signage doesn't include prior reminders that littering equals a $100 fine, no parking this side of the street, caution speed bumps, or blinking yellow lights warning drivers to slow down. By the time I've arrived at the round-about, I'm waffling between confusion and panic to remember the intersection cues to avoid collisions.

These abundant metal guides sometimes look like my well-meaning intentions. I appreciate fully engaging in projects, conversations, and goals. Instead of participating in a few quality endeavors, I want to submerse myself in all life offers. Like the excessive roadway signs, I may fill time and energy with an overload of sensory confusion. Instead of clarity, extra options can become detours or roadblocks if I don't use space discretion.

When I pay attention to only the as-sign-ments I need for my path, I'm able to maintain focused direction. My path resembles a more direct route than taking a round about approach to driving my life.

With my eyes on the road, watching for signals and signs,
Christina

LUMP OR LAMP?

I learned about inspecting feelings when they need "tempering" (aka attitude adjustment). The speaker who taught about evaluating emotions said that when there is a weight of depression, a person has reverted to thinking of a prior experience. When there is restless anxiety, a person is attempting to live in the future. This gauge offers me a quick way to reel me into the present moment. A side note, just how long is a moment?

I write this reflection from a phase of life where much moving and much holding is simultaneously taking place. I don't feel ready for the movements yet feel irritated by a holding pattern, according to my time table. To keep myself from warring between frustration and panic, I frequently use my journals as reference books. I peruse 2-3 months of journal entries and see, in writing, that circumstantial changes have occurred. Sometimes I simply forgot about key movements. I can either concentrate on the lump (setback) or choose to concentrate on the lamp of a lesson in front of me.

I picture the scene from *The Lion King* when Rafiki hits Simba on the head with his revelation stick. Simba knows he needs to return to his Pride Rock home to complete his leadership mission yet is stuck in the chasm between hesitation and restless yearning. Rafiki notices that the winds are changing and while Simba ponders the air shifts, Rafiki hits Simba in the head. When Simba questions why, Rafiki said the thump doesn't matter, it's in the past. He teaches Simba that sometimes one must go back to face the past but no matter what happened in the past, you can either run from it or learn from it. Rafiki swings at Simba again, but this time Simba takes the lamp (lesson) to his heart instead of another lump to his head.

What benefits do I receive by carrying the lumps of life instead of the lamps of lessons? Rubbing past lumps only distract me from the lamps lighting my future path. A genie will probably not appear when I rub the lamp, but the Lamp Lighter can fill me with hope and an invitation to look harder for His lesson. Rub the lump or rub the lamp?

Lord, help me use any lumps of my life only when they will teach me to move toward a future lamp lesson. Increase my desire to glance at the past as a land marker, but not a land mine. Guide me to be more aware of encouraging lamps and less focused on discouraging lumps.

Using my glasses for foresight and not hindsight, Christina

SHACKLES AND CHAINS

Trending now from someone making a prison bust.

Ironically, I work as a jail minister and while writing today's FROG blog, I was virtually slammed against a metal barred door of reality. I realized I've sentenced myself to a dank cell in Heart Attack Prison. I have a universal key, but I'm leaving it on the chain of my heart. Thoughts that began as innocent ventures ended in guilty convictions.

I recommitted to following Jesus' calling versus merely hearing or believing it. I've mentioned in previous blogs that my year's growth word is SIFT. I sifted distractions, evaluated spending and saving habits, focused on quieting external and internal noise. Through this sifting process, I (now) recognize I've allowed my heart to become hardened.

My pure intentions initially drew me nearer to God. I've digested sermons and books to learn to love God more. However, with a nearly obsessive quest to be an on-fire follower, I became blinded to other relationships and opportunities. I bought a lie that said to eliminate every distraction or obligation that didn't appear to be God's work.

Like a burglar's mask, sometimes God's prospects are disguised. God may see my sifting process as laundering His resources. What about using money to buy counterfeit lies that say I can appeal God's ruling over my life? Whenever I break and enter God's building of my earthly mission, I shoot holes in my heart. That same heart is called to love and serve God and others, not a worldly prison sentence. I am free in Christ (Gal. 5:1) so my only incarceration is to take thoughts and motives captive.

I began the year with a steadfast desire to learn about God's heart. By tightening the reins over my laws of discipline (food, schedule, exercise, money, conversations), I hung a noose around God's laws of love. For a healthy heart, I starved the "bad" but also famished the "good." This inner suffering penalty could have been reduced if I had plea bargained against a hot head and cold heart.

This morning, I appeared chain free, but after an inner prison break, I uncovered cold cinder block cells in my Heart Attack Prison. My mind sounded like a slamming steel door and a heart noisier than any penitentiary cafeteria. A one-woman fight beat me up, leaving my soul's appearance virtually unrecognizable.

"Today, if you hear his voice, do not harden your hearts as you did in the rebellion" (Heb. 3:15 NIV). I *thought* I was hearing God's voice louder than ever about how to love. How was I learning more about God's love, but not using His lessons to complete His life sentence to love *and* serve?

Lord, please forgive me for allowing my heart to grow stony. Let this temporary boulder not become a stumbling block. You know my heart (1 Sam 16:7). Place Your borderline patrol against the barbed wire of my actions. Help me sift loving and serving others through Your filter, Christina

PRODUCTION LINE

I appreciate the value of organized details and applaud wisely crafted designs. I caution against over planning without production, intentions without action. Reading and researching have significance, but when does too much strategizing bleed into procrastination? What amount of stringent forecasting translates to missed opportunities? Someone said when anticipation to strategize outweighs action it's time to change strategies.

I understand that not every brilliant idea needs to be implemented, but how many assignments are lost because over thinking leads to delay? Some concepts require waiting but do we (we, including the person at this keyboard) drag our feet under the rationalization that circumstances don't align with our expectations (our, again, including the person typing the FROG blog). The wisdom lies in determining when we are supposed to wait, and when we are expected to plow forward.

Consider the profession of agriculture. There is much to learn about farming before someone puts his or her hand to the plow. The potential farmer has decisions about tending crops, orchards, animals, or a combination of producing. He or she assesses crop selection, land preparation, product market value, climate, and soil tests.

What happens if that aspiring agrarian buys land, equipment, animals, feed, and seed but leaves all purchases in barns and grain bins? When asked why the animals haven't been fed or seed hasn't been planted, the dream farmer responds that he or she will start an agriculture profession when it's warmer, cooler, sunnier, or after vacation. The farm land then remains fallow and the animals are laid to rest, all buried under a harvest of drawing board sketches.

The plot (of land) thickened but never took root beyond a field of dreams. Build it and they will come ('but we're not in Iowa anymore' serves a load of corn as its logical ration). The land line became a land mine, a bumper crop dream dying in a nightmare of planning without production.

Haggai 2:19 (NKJV), "Is the seed still in the barn? As yet the vine, the fig tree, the pomegranate, and the olive tree have not yielded fruit." The last sentence of that verse offers redemption after actions and words intersect: "But from this day I will bless you."

Lord, help me use wisdom when tending your field plans. Guard me from planting thoughts and saturating the dirt with watered down intentions. Teach me when to let land lie fallow, prepare me to plant crops according to your growing season. Show me when to till the soil, weed, and irrigate so I can share a bumper crop harvest with others.

Implementing without withering away, Christina

TURTLE WAX: HARD SHELL INSPIRATION

I got to cross paths with a lady who was sitting on a bench overlooking a pond, her bright purple bicycle propped against a bench. As I walked past her, our eyes connected, and we exchanged a comment about being outside to collect our daily dose of Vitamin D via sunshine. She added, "Plus I get some of my best ideas from watching these pond turtles."

I wish I would have paused longer to ask what insights she collected from our armor shelled friends. When I walked away, I was struck by the irony that I write *The FROG Blog, Lessons From a Lily Pad* and wasn't more in tune with these rock-hard smiling pond dwellers.

Circling the pond, I noticed how one turtle's shell resembled a soldier's pith helmet. Another turtle was moving with determination and an amused expression on his face. I wondered what his destination could be. A couple of hard-rockers seemed to impersonate Jimmy Buffett's beach-loving lifestyle as they sunned themselves on the sand. By the time I reached the place where I originally met the turtle watching lady, she had pedaled away.

I started another lap around the pond and came across an elderly couple also making their way around the "turtle observatory." The frail man and woman were slow paced, but the husband's loving expression for his wife was steadfast. Like the turtles, they were single-minded, smiled, and armored their mate with a protective arm around their waist and shoulder. A peaceful contentment in their eyes hinted that their home was like a turtle shell, carrying their hearts with each other wherever they went. They were soldiers living joyfully for each other despite their feeble physical condition.

This couple was following Ecclesiastes 9:9 (NLT) which says, "Live happily with the woman you love through all the meaningless days of life that God has given you under the sun. The wife God gives you is your reward for all your earthly toil." It doesn't instruct us to live quickly, but happily. Turtles carry their heart in their home. This elderly couple carry their home in their heart.

Creator of fast lessons from slower earthly dwellers, thank You for showing me how I have everything I need from the waters of Your pond. Help me appreciate when you call me out of my shell. Remind me to trust Your perpetual armor. Grow me to be more like a turtle who takes time to smile, sunbathe, swim, and walk, all with forward motion at a capable pace as defined by Your design.

With lessons from Turtle Wax and Eph. 6: 10-18 armor, Christina

FIG NEWTON

I received a timely confirmation from a fig tree parable. "A certain man had a fig tree planted in his vineyard, and he came seeking fruit on it and found none. Then he said to the keeper of his vineyard, 'Look for three years I have come seeking fruit on this fig tree and find none. Cut it down; why does it use up the ground? But he answered and said to him, 'Sir, let it alone this year also, until I dig around it and fertilize it. And if it bears fruit, well. But if not, after that you can cut it down" (Luke 13:6-9 NKJV).

Figs yield sweet fruit in the summer and can be dried and stored for future use. As a fan of Fig Newton fruit and cake, I appreciate those sweet dried figs preparing for their debut as cookies. (To honor Newton's law, I've noticed when I consume too many of those delicious gems, I add gravitational pull of my own to the earth)! Adam and Eve utilized the fig's leaf to expand their wardrobe as well.

Back to the FROG Blog's focus. Jesus used a fig tree to reference God's judgment. God is overflowing with grace and mercy but if a person (note to self) continues to reject their Creator, a pruning process follows. This type of prune is not referring to one of the fruits of the Holy Spirit!

In my book, *"Life's Too Short for Dull Razors, Cheap Pens, and Worn Out Underwear,"* I used a few pages to discuss a nearly 3-year schlepping in desert phase. God was present and teaching during those three years, but I allowed virtual camels and cactus-like circumstances to blind any promising mirage. Like the fig, I was dried up, but not necessarily sweet. God allowed my fruity yield to be stored for a later date. I share a characteristic with this biblical fig tree. We both spent three years not producing healthy fruit.

Since June, I've entered a 'later date' phase and God's orchard plans for my mission field are becoming more fruitful. My Creator mercifully and graciously waited for me to absorb the lessons from desert land. He transplanted my spirit and soul from sand to rich soil, rooted near fresher streams of thinking.

Father, thank you for cutting out the dead roots of a once shriveled heart. Guide me to resemble an abundant fig tree, continually harvesting sweetness while remaining content to be stored and used for Your future purposes. Protect me from being pulled down into a gravitational pit of dryness.

From a well watered lily pad, Christina

ATTENDANCE DOESN'T ALWAYS EQUAL ATTENTION

A lady who shares my favorite walking route paused this morning to ask what I do as my profession. She promised herself that the next time she saw me walking she'd gather the courage to stop wondering and ask me how I used my days. She explained that she was fascinated to hear my answer because she frequently sees me wearing comfortable but stylish dresses walking with a contemplative expression blended with peaceful thoughtfulness.

I thanked her for her detailed observation and caring enough to ask. When I told her I am an author, life coach, and editor, she exclaimed, "I wish I had interesting jobs like that before I retired from 45 years as a machinist." It was my turn to be intrigued by how she interpreted her career and perceived mine. She said when she was in school, math was her least favorite subject, so she was surprised when she spent her life working in a precision driven math related field. She loves to read but all research jobs she wanted required post high school education and she didn't want to pursue continuing education.

I anticipated her reasons for not pursuing future certifications may be age or finance related. She explained that she had twelve years of perfect attendance but collectively probably less than a full year of perfect attention. Schools physically housed this lady but mentally she created a homeless shelter for her attention status. She didn't make excuses or hold regret for her lack of attention in formal classrooms. She simply appreciated how she was able to faithfully work as a machinist while being able to turn her detailed attention toward hands-on learning.

Attendance and attention. How often do I show up for morning quiet time physically present but spiritually and mentally absent?

My Teacher is present, but His student daughter is lost in thought about what happened yesterday and what may happen today. He is my Lead Machinist and I'm tooling around talking shop in my own mind!

This lady was sensitive to pay attention to her walking route surroundings. Her alertness created accessibility between us that wasn't originally detected. A familiar faced "stranger" left as a new acquaintance named Janice (and her dog Zoe) because we both paid attention to our surroundings. I was awakened by her inspirational lesson to pay attention to my Professor who is in continual attendance. I need His ongoing education no matter what profession I hold.

Teacher, please unite my attendance to my attention. Align my responsiveness with Your presence. Like Janice's alertness, give me courage to act upon my observations.

With heightened awareness, Christina

SPEND OR INVEST?

I recently met with a financial advisor to discuss retirement funds. He asked questions about spending habits and past investment practices. After I left our meeting, I used his financial tool teaching to leverage thought about spending and investing mental resources.

Do I tally my thinking as carefully as I budget my dirty green paper? What percentage of my brain waves are spent on fluff compared to investing in quality thinking that will offer a greater return? Am I regularly depositing my time in worthwhile projects?

That reflection led me to mentally diversify my portfolio by factoring relationships into the mix. Am I spending energy on liquid interactions or investing in valuable long-term growth relationships? Am I receiving substantial friendship dividends? Sometimes these liquid interactions could fertilize a seed in someone that pays off in heavenly dividends. Relationships matter to our Creator and I am reminded to invest in His Kingdom of people.

In the money market, my financial advisor discussed time guidelines and number projections. My birth certificate doesn't have an expiration date or projected age to "cash-out my life insurance policy." That fact encourages me to aggressively guard my assets against conservative living. I want to lavishly invest in others and spend minimal time living passively.

Spending my earthly time to be fully vested eternally, Christina

CAR LOTS AND REJECTION SLIPS

A fellow author visited our home and pointed out the simplicity in which I decorate (one small picture shelf, one wooden cross and one small framed inspirational quote on one wall). She wondered if I've always been a minimalist and if I've ever had a collection of anything. I jokingly responded that I've recently been collecting "unresponsive publication notices" (aka rejection slips). I've submitted more freelance writing to publishers and therefore, the more I write, the odds increase that all responses will not include publication. It's like the writer's law of averages using the marketing technique that the more you buy the more you save.

This author responded to my collection comment with gentle consolation, but I got to impart my Dad's resiliency lesson from the not-yet-published days of my writing career. We were on a car lot shopping for my next vehicle. Dad knew about my most recent "unresponsive" publisher notice and used our car shopping experience to draw a connection. Conversationally paraphrased, Dad said, 'Your writing is like a car purchase. Authors' work is an editor's car lot and they visit their submissions like we are comparing models, colors, options, and quality of a vehicle. You may choose one vehicle (story) today or you may take more time (notification delay). We may check out other car lots (authors), and we may investigate other styles. When you choose one of these 100's of vehicles, it doesn't mean the other cars are inferior. Your decision simply means you chose the one that fits your needs, budget, space in the garage (publishing space) for this time. Like an editor or publishing house, you won't buy only one car (article) in your lifetime'.

That wise choice lesson can be used with any other product that has more than one option. When there are 31 flavors of ice cream and you have a one scoop decision, the other 30 flavors aren't substandard. It means your taste buds reflected that preference for that visit. Dad's five-minute lesson increased my law of averages for resiliency. Instead of using the term "rejection letter," I prefer to say, "The editor chose a different vehicle" or "The publishing house decided on an alternative ice cream flavor."

Editor of my life help me serve with excellence and not be thrown off course when a person or business dismisses my work. Help me understand that my work does not equal my worth. You have taught that I cannot be separated from My Creator's love (Rom. 8:35-39). Guide me to respond as Jesus instructed, "And if anyone will not receive you or listen to your words, shake off the dust from your feet when you leave that house or town (Matthew 10:14 ESV).

Signing off as a possession minimalist seeking a wisdom maximalist, Christina

ENCORE OF 23 ARTISTS

The following reflections represent individual artists sharing their Fully Rely On God story. To maintain authenticity of the artists' craft, I have asked editors and publisher to limit changes to spelling and print formatting.

These stories, individually and collectively, have opened me to a broad spectrum of emotion and thinking. I'm intensely grateful for each artist's honesty. My only desire is that you, the reader, will find something deeply personal or similarly touching. Be ready to laugh, cry, and see God in the heart of these stories.

That First Step
Lyrics by Kelley Smith
Music by Michael Wayne Smith

In a church service one night on the Tennessee/Mississippi line, my husband Michael was singing an invitation song. I noticed a lady on the very last row holding so tightly to the pew in front of her.

I didn't know the lady or her circumstances, but as I prayed she would make her way down front, God said these words in my spirit: "THAT FIRST STEP." If she would just take that first step out of the pew and follow. Through the course of that night and the next couple of days, God gave me these words:

Maybe you came here alone, or to satisfy a friend.

You're feeling overwhelmed by the circumstance you're in.

You don't have to tell your story, there's no need to explain,

Just let go of that pew and you will never be the same.

Just take that first step, it's easy after that.

Just take that first step and there will be no turning back.

When you call out his name, you will never be the same,

Leave all your fear behind and take that first step.

You're feeling a little restless and your heart is beating fast,

See Jesus calls to you saying, "Come, don't be last"

He can change your life today, no need to run anymore.

He will give joy and peace that is waiting in store.

Just take that first step, it's easy after that,

Just take that first step and there will be no turning back.

When you call out his name, you will never be the same,

Leave all your fear behind and take that first step.

Kelley Smith's primary mission is to her husband and their two daughters Kerri and Kasey. She and Michael Wayne Smith have been married 26 years and reside in Oak Ridge, TN. She has an amazing testimony of how God healed her of a facial nerve condition called Trigeminal Neuroglia. She suffered with constant pain from this illness for 2 ½ years, but through God's grace and many faithful believers praying, she was healed in January 2014! Many times, during this period, she was tempted to give up rather than stand on a stage and encourage people. However, both Kelley and Michael knew there was a purpose for this trial and they have seen how God used her illness to encourage and challenge others. She chooses to use her pain to bring Him glory!

Mirror, Mirror
By Rain Noquisi

Once upon a time. A fairy tale. Little girls aspire to have a "Happily Ever After." Life happens. Rosy glasses are cast aside and reality isn't as wonderful and perfect as it once seemed. At times I wish I could go back and tell myself, "Don't!" That thought would change everything about my life today, so I keep that thought tucked away to the point of banishment.

My world is imperfect. My children are my world. Why would I want to take them away? My heart was broken but I have a new Person. He loves me intently. He pursued me like no other. Why on earth would I give Him up? I have a job and sure, it isn't where I want to be, but it is a stepping stone in the right direction.

Mirror, Mirror

I see so much in its smooth surface
Age has begun to add some flair to
the girl looking back.
She no longer has thick locks
or youths perks.

On the wall,
on my car,
sitting on my dresser.

I see this woman now.
She is somewhat tame.
More in-Love.
Crazy if you push the wrong buttons.

Hanging behind the door,
and medicine cabinet entrance.

She is strong, brave, and resilient.
She has come so far.
There behind her, are whispers.
Old habits that she fights sometimes daily.

Puddles and store front windows mimic your nature.
One simply can't escape you.

In her eyes there is still a wildfire
sometimes brimming with tears.
Unrealistic expectations slamming down
along with memories of the days of past.

Ponds UN-rippled,
fluid in a cup,
your doppelgangers
all of them.

Don't mock me!
I have come so far!
Don't show me that little rag doll of past!

Glass shatters,
swept away.
Liquid ripples,
dries up.

Sometimes those slivers and moist vapors try to come back.
Try to haunt me.
I just shake my head and laugh.

I'm imperfect and I am enjoying my unhappily ever after. I know I
will make more mistakes but I have learned a few things along the
way. Remember, you are beautiful and unique. Your past is always

behind you. Time can be your friend. It brings Wisdom, Strength, and can be very Kind. Don't get stuck on the negative.

I know it may be hard, but read my words. I pray you feel a bit of Peace that you are not alone. Little Princesses across the world, we all hope for Prince Charming and have all these fantasies of perfection. Dreams can be shattered hearts, broken to unbelievable depths. Don't lose Hope. Fight for yourself. Live for a better you. Strive to be the Queen. Tell the darkness your Light is brighter. Be the storm that takes the world by surprise.

From one Warrior Princess
to Another,

Rain Noquisi

From the fresh beaches of the Carolinas to the rugged mountains of the Appalachians, Rain continues to believe the good in everyone as she continues to grow from the timelines that made her. Out of place, or perhaps places to be in, she enjoys helping others and cherishes the moments provided to each of us, no matter how small. May her words and energy provide you a little peaceful solace, perspective, and Love.

The Scent of Hope
By Maryann Briggs

Christmas 2000 was spent with my parents, who traveled from Michigan to Tennessee to celebrate a most holy season. Festivities were enjoyed, and all the beautiful wrappings of a joyous occasion returned to their cupboards, and my parents were back in the snowy north.

Speaking with my mom a week after her visit, she told me she had the flu. As a nurse, I instructed her to force fluids, eat what she desired and rest. The next week, she could not shake that flu.

I asked my husband if he would drive me to Michigan with our two young children then pick me back up in a week once I was able to get Mom back on the road to recovery. Oh, that was a great plan of mine, but I was not prepared for what the real plan of life would be.

My father and I took Mom back to the doctor who ran more in-depth labs which indicated elevated liver enzymes. Next came a liver scan, her liver showed numerous spots, indicating cancer. Things picked up speed and she had the usual assortment of tests, looking for the "C presence" throughout her precious body.

I privately prayed, pleading that this was not really happening. Someone may call my prayers, panic prayers. I wasn't asking God for anything, I was just rambling and not really focusing on anything other than, "Make this all go away."

Test after test proved to worsen an already bleak picture and part of her colon was removed. After Mom's surgery I was sitting on her bed quietly reading her a meditation about The Great Physician. I stopped reading for a moment, remembering Mom had a hospital roommate. From the other side of the curtain, a voice said, "Please finish reading." The voice of Mom's roommate was

God's encouragement to me, to each one of us in that room. I knew He was present and with us, never once did I doubt this.

We brought Mom home and I stayed with her in the small den of their home. She would want to sit up at night on the side of the bed. As I sat next to her, she would lean all her weight on me, and we just sat together, so close, so loving, but not much talking.

She never let on that she knew she was dying, and I selfishly played along. It was a mother-daughter bond. Oh, we both knew the truth, but for the sake of crushing the other, we kept the secret of her pending heavenly travels to ourselves, never to discuss, but to take only to God in our private prayers.

The nights became longer with more struggles for her. Her breathing become more erratic and I prayed with great strength for God to spare her and not let things become unbearable. I begged Him to release her from suffering.

I received no response that could hear His words, but I smelled a rose scent unlike I have ever smelled before. The rose fragrance was so potent that it hushed me off to sleep, as if it was angel dust.

The next morning, I woke and looked around the room at the only flowers present. I bent down to smell the bright pink azalea, knowing it must have been those buds that shared their beauty with me for much needed comfort. There wasn't a trace of any scent.

God's revelation of His presence, a perfect rose in a way only I would recognize. No booming voice, no sure thought, not even a whisper. A rose, the purest of scents. My husband returned to pick me up, not after a week, but after 7 weeks and my dearest mother's funeral. I F.R.O.G.

Maryann Briggs is a wife, mother and RN, living in South Carolina. Her greatest career accomplishment is guiding and loving her two faith-filled children. Her son is a physician and her daughter is beginning graduate school in Oxford, England. Maryann enjoys gardening, walking, and being with her husband, family and friends.

Things You Don't See
By Rhea "RheaSunshine" Carmon

I struggle daily to understand my place in this world

Trying to motivate the youth of tomorrow to be greater

Than the latest YouTube challenge or tweet

I feel pain constantly and don't speak

How will I know that each day I have done the right thing?

To raise two boys, more beautiful than my imagination could have fathomed

I wonder if I love perfectly or even if it's possible

I can't always hold my bladder

And I feel pain constantly and don't speak

I'm tired of being superwoman

I have grown weary of the constant clamoring for my time, energy, and talent

I want to sleep more hours than I want to be awake

Fatigue has become something I brush off like lint

It's just going to be there, so I may as well forget about trying to get rid of it

I don't always feel beautiful, but I always feel worthy

I am better than I have ever been and worse all at the same time

I don't understand and I'm not always right

I feel pain constantly and don't speak

I am worried that there isn't enough time to teach them all I have

I would rather be at home than anywhere else in the world

I have MS and it causes some bad days that I don't tell you about

Because the truth is, if what was in my head came out

Everyone would be afraid

Because sometimes all I feel is rage

I feel pain constantly and don't speak

So pain has become my peace

Because more than anything, I appreciate consistency

I hide behind poetry because on the page I am free

And these are the things that I know

But you don't see

RheaSunshine hopes to touch hearts and inspire people to scribe their own stories. She is evolving from her beginnings in the world of slam poetry to becoming a well-known creative and prolific writer. She has authored three chapbooks and has recorded three audio CDs. Not motherhood, MS, or any obstacle can slow this Renaissance woman down. As she states in her writing, she still has poems that she hasn't even written yet.

Believe

By Lisa Celius

Every day I try to make you wrong

If I could just believe it then I might just get through it

But everyday there something so amazing

A little piece of you, somehow comes shining through

And I realize I can't believe

God put you on this earth to be with me.

Your smile is as bright as morning sunlight

It warms me to my soul, it found my heart, it made me whole

I'm fighting this with all that I have in me

You don't give up on me, and still you make me see

That I realize I can't believe

God put you on this earth to be with me

I'm terrified of all you've given to me.

This smile that's on my face, how you're making my heart race

You're breaking down the walls I built around me

And now it seems alright; it's not for me to fight

Now I realize I must believe

God put you on this earth to just love me

Lisa Celius is a healthcare application analyst by day, creative vampire at night. She is mother to four sweet dogs who love to watch her crochet and write. You can visit her craft website at *https://www.etsy.com/shop/HomemadeLovebyLisa*

Not my will but yours be done
By Elliot Consoli

At the turn of adulthood I had my comfortable little world rocked and shaken in a way I could never have anticipated. An avid distance runner, a bit of a health nut (especially for a high schooler), and coming from a family of pristine genetics, I was diagnosed with a chronic bowel condition one month before starting college, after losing close to 20 pounds and almost ending up in the hospital.

Why? On a physiological level it was undoubtedly a side effect of an aggressive acne drug that I had taken. But on a spiritual level? This was the question I was truly asking: why would God ask for me to suffer through this illness?

I had no answer at the time, which only plunged me deeper into the tribulation of having everything in my life turned upside down all at once. Family, friends, familiarity? All that was three hundred miles away, nowhere to be found on a foreboding college campus. Interests, habits, self-image, identity? Those were all gone too, left behind in the wake of an illness I did not know how to handle alone which left me more alone than I had ever been.

Why? I did not know. But that is precisely where God wanted me to change my life in a way I could not have imagined.

With nowhere to turn, no support network, no escapes, I almost had no choice but to turn towards the Lord. I had a powerful encounter with Him, where I realized the simple yet all-encompassing truth that He loves me, even loving all the things I couldn't bear to love in myself. He made me for Himself, and He was calling me back home. And I began to really love Him, too.

Over the next several years my life took a trajectory. Striving to place God at the center of my life, I was quickly surrounded by men of God who challenged me to grow into the best version of myself. I faced the daily pursuit of virtue in battling to balance my academic, social, and spiritual lives with a chronic illness that demanded much of me. I fell short and fell back on God's grace, and He picked me up and led me onward.

In a word, I changed. The old man was steadily being replaced by the character of Christ. And I began to see that if I wanted to become like Him, I must live like Him, and that required taking up the daily cross and following His servant example.

"My son, do not disdain the discipline of the Lord, or lose heart when reproved by him; for whom the Lord loves, he disciplines; he scourges every son he acknowledges" (Hebrews 12:5-6).

To this day the Spirit's words through Paul are my comfort and my strength. Through suffering, through illness, through trial, I was given the opportunity each day to become the man God asks me to be. While becoming a new man, I met a beautiful and loving woman, and she joined my side in the battle for holiness until our hands joined in the Sacrament of Marriage. Together we give our lives, first to the Lord, then to each other, and then in ministry to all who long to hear the call of a God who loves them more than they love themselves.

We struggled with a new burden of infertility and unceasingly lifted our prayers and sufferings to the God who hears us. And soon, we will give our lives to a little child who will learn just like we did that she has a Father who loves her."For this momentary light affliction is producing for us an eternal weight of glory beyond all comparison..." (2 Corinthians 4:17).

None of this would have been possible had God not broken into my 18-year-old life and blessed me with an illness that drastically changed the course of my life. I know that my limited ambitions would have resulted in a much less fulfilling life than what God's plan has now given to me. I have been blessed to see the fruits of my trial, and for that, I will be forever grateful. Through all the blessings, my illness has continued to affect me every day. God has not chosen to remove the burden, but instead, it presents me daily with new sufferings I must face and challenges I must overcome.

It is tempting to question why God won't heal me now, now that I've learned my lesson, now that I've given my life to Him and seen abundance of blessings in my life. As much as I struggle to bear this illness every day, if I am being rational and honest with myself, I must admit I wouldn't want it any other way. As challenging as it is for me to believe that statement, I know it is true, and I know I must trust in God's great plan. Because now I know the answer to my question – why does God allow us to suffer? Because, while He brings good through all things, it is only possible that the greatest good can come through the greatest suffering.

"For it was fitting that he, for whom and through whom all things exist, in bringing many children to glory, should make the leader to their salvation perfect through suffering" (Hebrews 2:10).

God Himself, in his infinite wisdom, chose to redeem humanity on a cross. The greatest love, the most valuable gift, could only be proven through suffering and sacrifice. There simply was no higher way for God to bless humanity. The weight of His sufferings became infinitely meritorious.

The Author of Life knew well what he was doing when he chose to die. He gives me this choice, too. Will I let my plans, my dreams, my will, die, in order that His glorious will be done, and to be blessed, indeed, far beyond my limited imagination? Like our Savior, we too must accept the hardship and trial in order to give and receive the greatest of gifts.

Faced with such suffering, I don't know if I would have the strength to choose it on my own. But paradoxically, "when I am weak, then I am strong" – because burdened and crippled by an illness I did not choose, with no way to stay standing on my own, I can choose to stand in Christ, and when I fall, He will lift me up again.

Suffering has given me a purpose, a wife, a ministry, a family, but most of all, suffering has given me Jesus Christ, and His Sacred Heart. I could have had a shadow of all this on my own. But God had greater plans, to break open my grasping hands and fill them with the most beautiful of gifts, the greatest of which is Him alone. In receiving this gift every day and continuing to suffer alongside His Son, I can only imagine the graces He has in store for us all.

Knowing this, I choose the greatest good, no matter the cost. I give up my plans and my comfort, O Lord, and you are not outdone in generosity. I could not choose you on my own, O Lord, and so You have made the choice, one I cannot live without. May the weight of my sufferings, united with Yours on the most holy Cross, bear eternal fruit for myself and my family, and may I never cease to choose You.

Elliot Consoli is currently pursuing full-time college ministry alongside his wife Abby. An avid runner, relentless problem-solver, and aspiring artist and chef, he strives to put his gifts in service of his family and others. He will soon transition to a professional career in order to be more present for his growing family and to support his wife in opening a photography business. You can check out their website and view the couple's latest adventures at veritatisphoto.com.

F- Our God is <u>FAITHFUL</u>
R-Our God <u>REIGNETH</u>
O-Our God is <u>OMNIPOTENT</u>
G-Our God is the <u>GREAT GOD</u>

By Janyce Gordon-Copney

While visiting Gatlinburg in 1979 I purchased a bumper sticker that read "I HAVE DECIDED TO FOLLOW JESUS." I did not realize that a drastic change was about to take place in my life. I didn't dare put that bumper sticker on my midnight metallic blue Trans Am. Instead I hid it in a bedroom, on a wall.

The following year my mother would be diagnosed with terminal cancer and would pass away. A friend purchased a wreath for my mother's grave which had a bible on it. I removed the bible, took it home, and started to read it.

God would water seeds that had already been planted in my heart even as a child. I decided to start attending a church. I was hesitant about the church my family attended. Women were told not to wear pants. God was calling me at that time in my life. I wore the pants to church anyway.

I didn't own a dress or a skirt. My job as a manager with KFC required me to wear pants. At this time in my life I would not allow a pair of pants hold me back. No way! I would accept Jesus Christ as my Savior and Redeemer.

A total turn around and upside down turn took place in my life. Before leaving Tennessee in 1982 I would lead friends and employees to Christ. And those who didn't make a declaration to Christ would at least have a God conscience.

One of my most memorable experiences in leading another person to the Lord was when I was working for Wendy's in New York. There was a teenager giving me such a run for my money. One evening I was in the office working on daily reports when suddenly the Holy Spirit fell like a blanket. I closed and locked the office door. I recognized this was a time to intercede in prayer. I prayed until the release came.

The next day the teen employee came in and was visibly upset. I asked her if she wanted to talk, she said yes. She was crying because she and her family would be moving to upstate New York. Since Christ and His love for her was the center of our conversation, I was able to lead the teen to a life in Christ. This young lady was the reason God sent the Spirit of Intercession the night before. Prayer was made for the teen to bring her into the sheepfold.

I continue to proclaim the name of Jesus no matter where I go.

Luke 9:26 (KJV)

For whosoever shall be *ashamed* of me and of my words, of him shall the Son of man be *ashamed*, when he shall come in his own glory, and in his Father's, and of the holy angels.

Revelation 19:5 (KJV) And a voice came out of the throne, saying, Praise our God, all ye his servants, and ye that fear him, both small and great. 6 And I heard as it were **the voice of a great multitude**, and as **the voice of many waters**, and as **the voice of mighty thunderings,** saying, **Alleluia**: for the Lord God **OMNIPOTENT REIGNETH.** 7 Let us be glad and rejoice, and give honour to him: for the marriage of the Lamb is come, and his wife hath made herself ready. 8 And to her was granted that she should be arrayed in fine linen, clean and white: for the fine linen is the righteousness of saints. 9 And he saith unto me, Write, Blessed are they which are called unto the marriage supper of the Lamb. And he saith unto me, These are the true sayings of God. 10 And I fell at his feet to worship him. And he said unto me, See thou do it not: I am thy fellowservant, and of thy brethren that have the testimony of Jesus: worship God: for the testimony of Jesus is the spirit of prophecy. 11 And I saw heaven opened, and behold a white horse; and he that sat upon him was called **FAITHFUL** and True, and in righteousness he doth judge and make war. 12 His eyes were as a flame of fire, and on his head were many crowns; and he had a name written, that no man knew, but he himself. 13 And he was clothed with a vesture dipped in blood: and his name is called The Word of God. 14 And the armies which were in heaven followed him upon white horses, clothed in fine linen, white and clean.

15 And out of his mouth goeth a sharp sword, that with it he should smite the nations: and he shall rule them with a rod of iron: and he treadeth the winepress of the fierceness and wrath of Almighty God. 16 And he hath on his vesture and on his thigh a name written, KING OF KINGS, AND LORD OF LORDS. 17 And I saw an angel standing in the sun; and he cried with a loud voice, saying to all the fowls that fly in the midst of heaven, Come and gather yourselves together unto the supper of the **GREAT GOD**; 18 That ye may eat the flesh of kings, and the flesh of captains, and the flesh of mighty men, and the flesh of horses, and of them that sit on them, and the flesh of all men, both free and bond, both small and great. 19 And I saw the beast, and the kings of the earth, and their armies, gathered together to make war against him that sat on the horse, and against his army. 20 And the beast was taken, and with him the false prophet that wrought miracles before him, with which he deceived them that had received the mark of the

beast, and them that worshipped his image. These both were cast alive into a lake of fire burning with brimstone. **21** And the remnant were slain with the sword of him that sat upon the horse, which sword proceeded out of his mouth: and all the fowls were filled with their flesh.

Janyce Gordon-Copney is married to a loving and caring husband Nathan. There is one son, Jeffery and six awesome grandchildren: Marquise, Tahmec, Dante, Jurrien, Blaise, and Lori Ann. Janyce added two furry children, Sophia and Sasha, to light up her family's home. More than anything, she looks forward to summers when she brings Blaise and Jurrien to Tennessee for two months.

My Life with Penguin
By Allisa D'Apice

I remember the first time that I brushed your beautiful, brown face. I was fourteen and you were four. I was yours, and you were mine. Galloping through a field turned my heart and soul free with the birds. It was the closest thing to flying that I'll ever experience.

I didn't ask for clothes or phones for Christmas. I asked for saddle pads and halters. Prom night wasn't spent in front of a mirror or in a fancy dress. Prom night was spent at the barn, cleaning tack and giving you a bath, as we got ready for a horse show the next day. While every girl in school got her senior picture taken in a gown, I had my senior pictures made with you. As I walked up the stage to receive my high school diploma, everyone in the crowd knew where I really wanted to be, as they read the words I created with athletic tape on top of my graduation cap, "I'd rather be riding."

I didn't leave you behind when I left for college, over a thousand miles away. I took you along. I didn't pick my summer jobs where I could make the most money or have the most fun. I chose my summer jobs where you could come with me.

You were such a talented jumper and an extraordinary athlete! Of the hundreds of horses that I've jumped, you were the absolute best! One in a million! I had the chance to sell you, for what seemed like an exorbitant amount of money, to a rich girl from Connecticut. I didn't even tell her that I'd think about it. I didn't hesitate when I told her, "There's no amount of money I'd take for him. He's priceless."

One of the most beautiful sounds in the world, to my ears, was the sound of your shod hooves clip clopping on a road covered with crunchy, Vermont leaves. My greatest memories were our 4 a.m. rides that we took by moonlight in Vermont, on roads covered with

174

freshly fallen snow. Roads touched by no one and no cars. We rode by total trust if the moon wasn't out. Your breath blew out in giant puffs of steam, hanging in the cold, morning air.

You always made me laugh when you dunked your face in the water trough, not just to your muzzle but all the way in; all the way in and past your ears! And then you would let the water dribble on my shoulder or shirt. You nickered your greeting, in a low tone, every time I went to the barn.

We won just about every class that we entered because nobody saw my cues to you. I didn't have to give any. Together, we just knew what we needed to do and when. We spent the last ten years of your life riding bareback with just a halter and lead-rope. We still found fallen trees to jump and galloped together, with my arms wide open, because we trusted each other. Your mane caught every tear that I shed as I cried about life and then we'd ride the troubles away. You were the first one to know about everything happening in my life, the good and the bad.

The tears that I cry now have nowhere to go because you are gone. I can't believe that I have lost my best friend, my daily companion for twenty-six years. A piece of me is buried with you, Penguin. I'm happy for you that you did not suffer. I'm happy that you chose a beautiful, final, resting place under the tree, up on the hill where you used to stand in the pasture and wait for me. I love you, Penguin. I will miss you every day for the rest of my life.

All things bright and beautiful. All creatures great and small. The Lord God made them all.

Allisa D'Apice is an active, homeschooling mother and manages a successful independent insurance agency with her husband in Dunlap, TN. She and their three children continue to provide a forever home to four dogs, four cats, two horses, two Vietnamese

Pot-Bellied pigs, and assorted laying chickens; all which were rescued from abusive and/or neglectful situations. Allisa no longer has the desire (or time) to ride horses. She enjoys serving as Assistant Scoutmaster for her son's Boy Scout Troop, coaching her kids in soccer and providing endless rides to their endless other activities.

Passing on Wisdom

By Dave Dutrow

We got Firehouse to bring home for dinner one Wednesday night. Kids eat free on Wednesday's, so this is a relatively normal occurrence for our family. As we drove home, Kelsey (my three-year-old) said she wanted her drink so she could drink some of it on the way home. Katie (my nine-year-old), that night's designated drink holder, said, "No you don't. I used to drink most of my drink before we got home, and then I would be jealous when everyone else had a drink and I was drinking water. Don't make the same mistake I did."

I love that my older girls teach their younger sisters life lessons! We all have learned lessons the hard way over the course of our lives. How often do we impart that hard-won wisdom on to the next generation? Maybe even more importantly, how often do we seek out wisdom from those who have traveled our current path before us?

I talk to my parents nearly every day on the way to work. It gives us a chance to keep up to date with what is going on in our respective lives, but it also gives me a chance to get advice on problems I am experiencing. Sometimes those problems are related to my girls (I have three), sometimes it is a work issue. At times, I just want to hear a different perspective from someone who is close to the issue but not *too* close, if you know what I mean.

And just like my girls, when I receive advice on a particular issue, there are times that I heed that advice. Other times I take their advice in and decide to move in a different direction. My parents understand that. They don't get offended if they advise me on something and I go another way. We all have to live our own lives and make our own decisions.

It is always a good idea to get as much wise input as possible before making decisions (particularly big, important decisions). For those important life decisions, we need to get input from God through prayer. We also should seek wise counsel of those whose judgment we trust on matters both big and small. When we seek out and receive this counsel, we are more likely to make sound decisions.

That evening in the car, Katie looked out for her younger sister. Kelsey was not happy in the moment, but she appreciated it at dinner when she still had a full drink in front of her to go with her sandwich and Doritos. Being three years old, she didn't thank Katie for preserving her drink, but I think she took that little nugget of information and stored it away for future use. My bet is that at some point in the future, Kelsey will be able to make that wise choice on her own because of the counsel she received from her older sister. I pray that we will all seek out and accept wise counsel in all our endeavors.

My son, pay attention to my wisdom, turn your ear to my words of insight, that you may maintain discretion and your lips may preserve knowledge.

Proverbs 5:1-2

Dave Dutrow is a Naval Academy graduate and nuclear engineer. None of his education and experience prepared him for his greatest adventure: father of three girls. His girls are aged 17, 9 and 3. If you do the math (and Dave has), you will discover that he will have a teenage girl in the house for twenty consecutive years. He has chronicled many of the adventures of his family on Facebook, and those anecdotes form the basis of his published book, Caution Ahead: 94 Tips to Navigate Parenting. He is looking forward to a lifetime of learning more lessons from his girls, and possibly sharing those lessons with others, so they can learn from his experiences.

As Delivered
By Michael ("Tig") Eder

Individual circumstances may be different, but the desired end goal is the same. For prodigal children, I want them to come back to us and God quickly. I want overnight success of healing and overall well being.

The truth I must accept is, the time before and after their return is incomprehensible to me, but not unknown to God. The severity of what the children have gone through and need to go through is also unknown to me. The time to heal after their return requires me not to quit, to keep praying, no matter how difficult it may become at times.

There is an understanding of God's love when my kindness replaces anger. That understanding comes to me with an element of surprise. I also understand there may be a relapse to the prodigal lifestyle after a child has returned to God. I pray this will not happen, but need to remember that people operate under free will.

In his letter to the Romans, Paul wrote: "Therefore receive one another, just as Christ also received us, to the Glory of God" (Rom 15:7). I must receive and accept our prodigals in whatever state they are in upon return. Their return might be in person, by phone, email, or even social media. The method, time, and place of their return is not up to me and I need to be ready to accept them "as delivered" by God.

Michael "Tig" Eder is an Insurance Director by trade. He's President and Founder of Roll As You Are Inc (RAYA), lifetime car enthusiast, father, "Grampz", and husband to the wonderful author of this book.

Author's note: Tig allowed me to edit every part of his submission, but asked that his bio remained as written. (He understands that extra oatmeal chocolate chip cookies are not included for charming brownie points)!

The Long, Slow Journey to Answer the Call
By Beth M. Erickson

In 1988, at 17, uncertain of my future, I met a charming, charismatic black Catholic nun named Thea Bowman in Washington, D.C. We were being honored as American Cancer Society Courage Award winners from our home states–hers Mississippi, mine Wisconsin. My cancer had been in remission for eight years. Thea was in a wheelchair due to advanced cancer.

My family and I had a connection with Thea because my great aunt was also a Franciscan Sister of Perpetual Adoration. That week, we helped Thea get where she needed to be as she was traveling alone. In return, she gave me direction. She told me that I would major in English, and that I was going to teach.

Well, if there was one thing I knew, it was that I would not teach. I had spent enough time in school, a miserable place wherein someone who had been through cancer and lost friends to the disease never seemed to fit. I did take a bit of her advice though and majored in English, seeking marketing communications internships that led me toward a successful career in thermoplastics, medical, and university settings. I had lofty goals: getting awards, promotions, and recognition, which I did. However, I was never happy in my job.

Years later, shortly before my husband and I adopted children, an opportunity to freelance emerged. I said, "Yes!" I was relieved to work on my own, building my career to eventually edit four publications, development edit books, create other projects, and win an award or two for my writing and marketing work.

I was content, but not happy. After 10 years or so, despite the small business success, my husband wanted me to get a full-time job so our family could get a better healthcare plan. His company's plan was not fantastic. I resented giving up what I had built, but explored possibilities. After one promising interview, I left knowing I had aced it and the job would be an excellent fit with my skills and offer great benefits.

But the thought of an 8 a.m. to 5 p.m. job was stifling. More than that, when I thought about missing some of our children's school functions and doing healthcare PR for 40 hours a week, I grew downright depressed. I withdrew my name from consideration the next day. I now knew what I *didn't* want. I also knew that I needed to ease into this full-time thing.

Six months later, I read about the death of Carol, the mother of a dear friend from high school. My heart broke for my friend, with whom I reconnected at the funeral. This was a gift, the kind of gift her mother would have bestowed on us. Carol oozed warmth and hospitality and genuinely cared about others.

The evening of the funeral, around 9 p.m., I felt a sudden, inexplicable urge to look online for a job. I explored LinkedIn as a source for the first time and found a job for a part-time Education and Investment Specialist, involving regional travel to educate people about their retirement plan. Though I didn't have financial or retirement plan experience, I applied—after all, it said, "experience preferred, but not necessary."

After a five-step interview process, including giving a presentation, I was hired. Though it has not been an easy road, and the learning process was a bit like being thrown into the water to learn to swim, it has been a Godsend in my life. Nearly two years later, I was asked to take on a full-time role, and I said, "Yes!"

So what do I do now? I teach. I have learned that educating others is exhausting *and* rewarding, and you don't have to do it in a school setting. In this job, I have been reminded that I have value and potential and work can be fun. I have learned that you *can* find a company where ethics matter and the culture *is* about doing what's best for clients. I have learned that life is never about my goals. It is *always* about helping others meet theirs.

Answering the call to teach has been long and slow, because I was stubborn and blind. I didn't recognize what others saw in me. Angels in my lifelong journey, like Sister Thea and Carol, have gently guided me toward the inevitability of the call and the gift of its answer. It only took me 23 years to listen!

Beth M. Erickson is a retirement plan relationship manager who has worn many hats in her life. From writer and editor, to poet and producer, to mother and wife, to friend, she sees life as a gift. She has been thoroughly blessed by the wonderful people in her life.

God Brought Me to My Knees
By Erin Ferowich

Rejected, alone and scared. There were years of isolation, depression, loneliness, sadness, buried in desperation and hopelessness. There was no way out. From darkness to light, this is my story of surrender.

I was 25 years old, raised Catholic with well involved parents. I am the oldest of four, the responsible one. I went to private school until 8th grade. At this time, I look back and see the rebellion building in me. I still speculate what the reasons were, yet there is no one moment to blame, no crisis or major identifying moment that has yet revealed itself to me.

I was young, naïve, innocent, and most called me sheltered. As the years of public high school went by I had many feelings that began coming out in my behaviors and choices. They were results of feelings that I did not understand. What I can identify now was pressure, fear, stress, anxiety, wanting to fit in, wanting to prove my worth, and most of all, a lack of self love.

For the most part, this manifested itself in a prideful attitude of strength and independence and I excelled in multiple sports teams. I gained respect in the small town I lived in and was loved and supported by many. However, I started making risky decisions that changed my surrounding crowd, and I sought something different than the goodness of life I had taken for granted. I didn't know it then, but it was a perfect storm waiting to happen. It just so happened these same years would later be called the beginning of a drug epidemic in this small town. Many friends today are addicted, in jail, or dead; sad to say, few made it out alive or became better for it.

I was 25 years old when I finally reached my ultimate breaking point and called my mom. She drove to pick me up and little did I know, I had just begun a new chapter, or really, a whole new book of life. From this moment, I had only one choice, I had to fully rely on God. I couldn't have even told you what this meant or who God was to me, but at that moment there was nothing anyone could do for me.

I was at rock bottom. I had dug myself in a hole mentally, physically, and emotionally. My family had surrendered me long before, yet, they were still there in my greatest time of need. This time was different than any time before that. Seven years in a vicious cycle of enslaved addiction kept me bonded, lost, hidden behind the bars I created in my own mind, and barriers that I built up in my heart.

My mom and brother drove me to Saint Augustine, Florida on December 27, 2011, and I never looked back. In Saint Augustine, I became a part of a religious community for women. There I learned to live a simple lifestyle of three pillars; prayer, work and friendship. The community was founded in northern Italy by a religious sister named Mother Elvira, who felt called to help addicts that are rejected and the youth that are hopeless. There, I learned about having faith and how to live a Christian lifestyle rooted in the three pillars; prayer, friendship and work.

It is through love of God and self, that we can love and serve others to give our life meaning and purpose. Every good act of love helps me to be free from the bondage of sin and become the newer and better version of myself. It was apparent over the years in the community that it was helpful to look at myself in the light of the truth behind character flaws or poverties, as well as deep rooted feelings that can be at the root of addiction.

Being in a new place, with new people, with the light of Christ in their eyes, with the same story as me, God placed hope in my heart. His mercy and graces flowed in to bless my half hearted yes that was really more of a weak no. I began to put my old self behind and begin anew. In awe of the changes in my heart, my love for my faith started to be renewed. I had nothing- no money, no clothes, no friends, no hope and no belongings, and God gave me everything.

I grew stronger, I opened my heart and I felt His love for me, and I started to pray again. The most important thing I received was the healing in the stillness of my heart and soul with the Lord. I realized I wanted to let go of my past, so I wrote down and confessed all of the wrong that I had done in my time away from God. He freed my heart, and led me through deep spiritual healing, which I really can't even explain in words. I remember the day He gave me back my joy. I remember learning to love and have compassion again for others. He showed me how to work on myself and learn from my mistakes, and how to continue to seek balance in all I do. My life has to be rooted in prayer and love for God and myself, and then in giving this love to others.

Today, I am 7 years clean and sober. My life has taken off and done a complete 360. I have been home to Tennessee multiple times over the years, and of the few people I have seen, they tell me they can't believe it. They all thought I was dead by now. I should have been dead, I should have been in jail, I shouldn't have survived, but I did.

I have been outside of the religious community for over 2 years and still in recovery, I am still healing. I spend time every day working on the person I want to be. I find quiet time for prayer that gives me peace and intention to follow God's will in my life. I try to be honest with myself and share openly about myself in friendship. I live my life to its fullest, which is my program of recovery and healing, of which I pray I never get tired of.

Darkness Into Light

the past, an all too distant memory
sometimes seems like yesterday-
but most times, it's so far away;
the gentle reminders, I don't mind anymore,
they help me remember when God's mercy
knocked down my door;
Even when I wasn't seeking,
undeserving, barely breathing;
I gave my broken yes, more like a
Heartfelt NO! to change the life I was leading,
yet all at once so ready to leave behind.
No I can't forget, nor ever regret
this life changing path
and how far I've come
on this journey of self awareness,
I have been so blessed-
to live with purpose and dignity-
to live fully in His love
until I get to Eternity.
by erin

Erin Ferowich is currently working part time while in college pursuing her goal of becoming a Physical Therapy Assistant. She resides in Saint Augustine, Florida and lives just a few minutes away from the beach. If this story touched you, or if you or your loved ones have any experience with addiction or miracles of hope

that have happened to you, please reach out to me at
Erin.ferowich@aol.com.

Cleansing
By Iris Long

After washing the dishes, I wiped off the countertops and appliances. Early afternoon sunlight filled the triple window above the sink, flooding the kitchen with cheerful warmth. I rinsed the dish rag and wrung it out, preparing to hang it on the sliding rack inside the cabinet to dry. I noticed a few specks on the cabinet door, which housed the small kitchen garbage can, and as I cleaned the door, inspiration dawned to wipe down all the cabinets. I progressed steadily around the modest rectangular kitchen in a leisurely manner, enjoying the pleasure of this simple task. My mind was quiet while my hands were busy.

The soft teal and white striped wallpaper above the cooktop, upon closer inspection, revealed small spatters. I leaned over the stove and with some effort scrubbed the surface. As I rubbed, I noticed more areas that needed cleaning including the grooves in the cabinet design, the corners where the trim pieces met, and the facing between the cabinet doors. The more intently I inspected the surfaces, the more dirt I discovered. I returned to the first cabinet door where I had started cleaning, and the grime I had not observed previously was now revealed under fresh scrutiny. Suddenly, I heard the Lord speak in my spirit. "Iris, when I reveal something dirty to you, it is not for condemnation; rather, I am working to cleanse you of what needs to be removed." My hand froze as He spoke and I stood still, replaying His words over and over in my mind.

I had been struggling lately, impatient for God's next move in my life, trying to understand what appeared to be an indefinite delay. There were a few occasions when breakthrough had seemed eminent, but nothing changed in my daily life, and the waiting resumed. Prayers about my future were met with promptings, instead, to pray for unrelated situations and people. I battled frustration, doubt, and weariness, while declaring my faith and trust in God and encouraging myself through His promises in the scriptures. I trusted His love for me and I was aware of His presence, but the questions persisted. He has been working in me for the past two years, replacing "self" with more of Him, transforming my heart and mind. Now, in an unexpected answer to my prayers, His divine scrutiny has exposed the need for deeper cleansing, and I must yield to the process before advancing.

I continued my work in the kitchen, using a stepladder to reach the upper part of the cabinets and the wallpaper on the soffit. My dish rag was grungy by the time I finished. The revelation from the Lord had settled in me like a warm fuzzy blanket, and I felt safe and secure. His love and peace filled me as I accepted His truth in silent surrender. Inspection of the surfaces I had cleaned revealed the wallpaper and cabinet doors gleamed brightly, and I smiled in response to my efforts. Deep contentment surged through my heart as I carried the ladder out to the garage. As I walked, I thanked the Lord for His profound words, confident once again that God will complete the work He has begun in me according to His purpose. I will rest in Him while He proceeds.

"⁵ I wait for the Lord, my soul waits,
And in His word I do hope.
⁶ My soul *waits* for the Lord
More than those who watch for the morning—
Yes, more than those who watch for the morning."

~ Psalm 130:5-6 NKJV

Iris is the author of "Showered By Grace", her first published book. Her journey recently included a return to Goshen, Indiana, where she currently resides. Read more about her true-life love story and follow her blog on her website www.irisundergrace.com.

The Importance of Believing in Something Bigger than Yourself
By Tricia McNamara

I was an inquisitive child, always asking a lot of questions, constantly curious about why things were the way they were, how they got that way, when it happened, and so forth. I'm sure I drove people nuts with my questions. It was important to me to have all the facts at my disposal, not just then, but now.

Knowledge can be empowering but so can faith. Growing up, my family went to church together every Sunday morning in Toledo, Ohio. My maternal grandparents (Dorothy and George), my parents (Bob and Margo) and my brother, Tim, and I dressed up and worshipped together. This strengthened not only our faith but our family bonds as well. I wouldn't trade those memories for the world.

After we worshipped together, my family would go back to my grandparent's house for Sunday supper. My grandmother, whom I lovingly called Gram, was a great cook. Sometimes, we would just have sandwiches from whatever my grandmother had on hand. She'd make ham sandwiches, real ham, not lunch meat, or round grilled cheeses made in a cast iron press like the ones people use today over camp fires.

One Sunday a month, Gram would pull out all the stops and whip up a delicious roast beef dinner with all the trimmings—mashed potatoes, corn, rolls, usually served to us on plates warmed in the oven. We would have salads on chilled plates and a delicious, usually chocolate, dessert. Gram made the best German chocolate cakes and cookies. To this day, I have never had a better meal than those roast beef suppers after church.

Whatever we ate, we ate it as a family and enjoyed our time together. The menu didn't matter so much as the fact that we were

193

sharing the experience as a family, something that gets taken for granted in today's fast-moving society. Eating together helped strengthen our family and gave us a sense of belonging to something bigger than ourselves.

Life is hard at times, a challenge to say the least. As I get older, I find it critical to have something bigger than yourself to help keep you grounded when chaos ensues. There will be times in life when your world will be rocked by unexpected death or disasters of one kind or another. You need to have a more powerful influence to provide strength when your own seems woefully weak or even completely depleted. For me, that is faith in God. God is my "something bigger than myself." It makes all the difference.

I was brought up Catholic, attended a Catholic school for ten of my twelve years of early education. My questions weren't always enthusiastically embraced but more often than not, they were answered for me along the way. Never one to give up when a question nagged at my heart, I often sought answers from the wisest woman I knew, my maternal grandmother. Not only was she my grandmother, but my best friend. I trusted her implicitly and learned a great deal from her teaching over the years.

Almost every Monday after school, I walked over to Gram's house where she and I would discuss the previous day's gospel readings. We discussed what it meant in our lives and life in general. We'd often read more from the passage to gain further clarity if I needed it. She was patient and clear in her explanations, knowing how important it was to teach me accurately in a way that my growing mind could grasp. Some of the most memorable talks I had with my grandmother were from those Monday afternoon talks about the Bible.

Gram taught me what the world left out, that there was something bigger than all of us out there and that it was critically important to grab hold of it, to grab hold of God, with both hands. Due to complications after a stroke, losing Gram was the single hardest thing I had ever experienced. It nearly broke me. My heart was shattered.

I put my life on hold and fought not to freefall into an abyss of despair. Like the infamous "Footprints in the Sand" tells us, "it was then that (God) carried me." I held on tightly to God, and my family until the despair lessened. Pain so deep never truly goes away. It can be managed. Pain has to be managed or it will consume you.

God has carried me many more times after that in my life. My husband of less than a year at the time was diagnosed with level 3, stage 4 skin cancer and given five years to live. Fortunately, he was saved by amazing doctors at the University of Pennsylvania. He's now fifteen years cancer-free thanks to God's amazing Grace and healing powers.

There are so many other times that God carried me through tough times—my mother's breast cancer that took her life way too soon; friends that succumbed to sickness; personal setbacks in finances and in careers. Through it all, I had no strength of my own other than what was given by something bigger than myself, by God.

I need a stronger, more powerful presence and God carries me with his love and strength, especially when I have none of my own. In my darkest days, I find solace knowing that he will always be there. My faith has been my salvation; that has made all the difference.

Tricia McNamara is an e-commerce business owner who resides in West Deptford, NJ. She is currently at work on her first fiction novel. She whole-heartedly believes that taking the "road less traveled" is the best option and tries to put it into practice on a

daily basis. Feel free to reach out to her at
jingleinjersey@yahoo.com.

A New Commandment
By Ron McPherson

"I give you a new commandment, that you love one another. Just as I have loved you, you also should love one another. By this everyone will know that you are my disciples, if you have love for one another." – John 13:34-35 (NRSV)

I just turned 55, and even though I'm a bit north of six feet and haven't weighed south of 200 pounds in what must be at least two decades, I have cousins who still call me "Little Ron." That's because my 86-year-old father will forever be "Big Ron" to them. As a kid, folks would say I was the spitting image of my father. I often tried to imitate him too. Dad smoked Dutch Masters. I "smoked" El Bubble – blue bubble gum cigars. I was a chip off the ole' block. If a receding hairline and a love for all-things-Bing Crosby count for anything, I still am. I suppose to some, I'll forever be "little Ron." They'll probably carve it in my tombstone.

C.S. Lewis wrote in *Mere Christianity*, "Every Christian is to become a little Christ." Without getting into the theological implications, the Cliff Notes version seems to be this: I'm supposed to be the spitting image of my Savior in such a way that others will be naturally attracted to him. For sure, people were attracted to Jesus when he walked the earth some two millennia ago. At least society's marginalized and outcasts were. The self-righteous religious crowd though? Not so much.

Acts 11:26 says, "It was in Antioch that the disciples were first called 'Christians'" (NRSV). Being a Christian then, what Lewis would call a "little Christ," is synonymous with being a disciple - a learner - which for me means there's no wiggle room on that love bit in John 13. Jesus commands it; it's not merely a suggestion. As a disciple, I should learn to love like Jesus loved, which especially includes the least of these.

For me, a disciple initially conjures up images of Jesus' apostles: Peter, Andrew, James, John, Matthew, Thomas, Judas (Judas wasn't much into that disciple thing though), and five others whose names escape me. At any rate, the apostles were disciples too, though they were a distinct, God-empowered group sent to deliver the good news accompanied with supernatural signs - cool stuff like performing miracles. I can't perform miracles, unless you count that time I successfully answered a three-pound hotdog challenge at a West Virginia eatery, or when I happily stuffed down 60 pieces of sushi after a particularly stressful day. The point is that Jesus' disciples were not limited to this inner circle of apostles. It wasn't that way then, nor do I believe it is to be that way now.

Jesus' words in John 13 seem almost counterintuitive to my preconceived notions of how a super saint is supposed to look. Jesus mentioned nothing about blue-ribbon church attendance being a test of authentic faith. Just my luck too, because I would put my record up against Enid Strict's anytime. Enid Strict is the Saturday Night Live Church Lady in case you're wondering. And if that name still doesn't ring a bell, you may know a church lady stereotype if you grew up in church. She was that "sweet" little gossiping lady who walked around with an over-sized Bible tucked under her arm, flicked you on the ear for whispering during the sermon, and always brought the Jell-O salad to the church picnics. Growing up Baptist, we called church picnics "fellowship meetings," which was code for all-you-could eat brownies and egg salad sandwiches.

Now back to that love thing in John 13. Apparently, religious performance didn't make Jesus' cut either, which should come as no real surprise considering this:

> When the Pharisees heard that he had silenced the Sadducees, they gathered together, and one of them, a lawyer, asked him a question to test him. "Teacher, which commandment in the law is the greatest?" He said to him, 'You shall love the Lord your God with all your heart, and with all your soul, and with all your mind.' This is the greatest and first commandment. And a second is like it: 'You shall love your neighbor as yourself.' On these two commandments hang all the law and the prophets" (Matthew 22:34-40 NRSV).

To Jesus' original hearers, the phrase *law and the prophets* meant their Hebrew scriptures, what we know as the Old Testament. Love for God and others was to undergird their entire view of the scriptures. I suppose no one needed a commentary when they heard that. My wife likes to say, "Plain talk is easy understood."

Notice also the John 13 passage mentions nothing about measuring Christian authenticity through intellectual adherence to a theological creed or denominational doctrine. Nary a word even mentioned about daily Bible reading either. (Don't I at least get points for reading all the way through Leviticus)?

The English language is not very precise in its use of the word *love*. I *love* my family. I *love* my friends and church small group. I also *love* college football and *The Andy Griffith* show. I *love* collard greens and sweet potato pie and lasagna and cheeseburgers and sushi and cornbread and ice cream and cheesecake and…ok, there's a recurring theme here, but you get the point.

The word *love* can mean several different things in our language. Greek, the language in which the New Testament was written, does a better job of distinguishing the various concepts of love. There is *Phileo* (affection or fondness), *Eros* (this one makes me blush, so you can figure this one out on your own), *Storge* (natural affection, as with one's family), and *Agapao* (unconditional, self-sacrificial, godly type love) – which just so happens to be the word used in the John 13 passage. This type of love is descriptive of the early church (Acts 2:44-47) which had no need for flashy programs or clever methodologies to grow its numbers. Instead, they just radically loved each other while God did the rest. And a lot of people wanted to be counted in the action. Turns out that Jesus was on to something in John 13.

Jesus tells his followers (that would be disciples) a couple of chapters later in John, "apart from me you can do nothing" (John 15:5 NRSV), which is especially comforting because I have a long way to go in loving others like Jesus did. I guess that means I must *F*ully *R*ely *O*n *G*od every step of the way to help me with this. Seems like I've heard that somewhere.

Ron McPherson is an Assistant Superintendent of a public school system serving over 60,000 students. Prior to that, he was the CFO of a Christian non-profit that helps prepare city youth to become godly leaders in their communities. Ron and his wife Stephanie reside in Knoxville, TN with their two adult sons, Brenton and Brock.

A Story of Love
By Bob Reuscher

"In the beginning, God created the Heavens and the Earth…" (Gen 1:20).

One of the greatest gifts we get from God is Love. God is love himself. The greatest gift we can return is to love him and others. "Love is patient; love is kind. It does not envy; it does not boast: it is not proud. Love does not dishonor others; it is not self-seeking; it is not easily angered; it keeps no record of wrongs" (1 Cor 13:4-5).

Margo, my wife and most precious gift from God, was lifted to the Lord ten years ago. She loved the Lord, she loved others. I know that God was there, holding her hand that peaceful night when he called her home to finally be with him. She was an amazing mother to our son, Tim, and our daughter, Tricia. We all miss her dearly. She will forever be loved and remembered as the very special lady that she was to all of us.

Many changes have taken place in our lives since the day Margo went home to the Lord. She left behind many precious memories. She left behind my children, my most precious gift from her and God. I have so many good memories of our life together, times of so much joy and happiness. I found a little white badge that was left in a box in her dresser. On it was written, "Love One Another." Thinking back on that, I firmly believe that this is the message of life that God wants us all to put into daily practice. She also left a hand written memo that said, "Good-Better-Best. Never let it rest until your Good is better and your Better is your Best."

I believe that you are happiest when you are true to yourself in doing what Jesus asked of us, what Jesus did and showed us in actions and in words while he was on this Earth. In reflecting on this, I am reminded how very much Jesus loves me and all of us. He suffered and died for us. "Greater love than this no man hath that a man lay down his life for his friends." "Love the Lord, your God, with all your heart and all your soul and with all your mind." "Love your neighbor as yourself."

Knowing how to be happy starts with a smile. Most smiles to others will usually get one in return. Hearts talk to hearts, no words are necessary. About 5 years ago, I was helping one of my next door neighbors trim some brush in her yard. In the middle of my lawn work, some good friends of mine came over and joined me. They extended their hands in a friendship that soon blossomed. We both have grown together in many ways since that time. They have taught me so much about what true Love is, to love God, how to care, and share with each other.

I am still on life's amazing and mysterious journey, still climbing to the top of the mountain in search of the peak and meaning of it all. With the help of the Lord and all of his helpers, the climb gets a little easier every day. The most rewarding aspect of my life's journey has been when I care for and help others when I can. Helping people is the best way to live a good life, providing you with inner peace and happiness as you give freely of yourself to another. Happiness becomes even better when you are at peace with yourself, a peace that comes from a gift from the Lord for doing what he asks of us.

Time is precious. Life is short. It is so important to follow the right path as we make our way through our lives. One of the most important lessons that I've learned in life is to always try to do good. A lady from my church reminded me how critical this lesson truly is. I spend my life trying to follow Jesus, sometimes succeeding, sometimes not, but always trying. I have been trying to be totally dependent upon God every day of my life. The last ten years of my life have been a mirror of the first 70—some moments good, some bad. I take life a day at a time, trying to grow a little better than the day before, living in the present, hopeful for the future.

Over the past few years, I've joined two e-mail prayer chains. The one from church has frequent requests for my fellow Christian's needs. The other is for county prisoners who request help, hope and healing for prisoners, compassion for the warden, staff, and volunteers. I've added my own daily prayer chain to include my family, neighbors, good friends and those who have people who have gone before us to meet the Lord.

Prayer is one of the most important things we can do, for ourselves, for others. We all need prayers. So many people in the world have nothing, have no one. So many need our prayers. Sometimes, people just need a hand up. Try to be that person lending a hand, dependable and encouraging as you do so, showing those who need the love of God through your words and actions.

There are many "true" religions in the world. We all seek similar answers from a Being larger than ourselves. We need to stop fixating on the differences and focus on the similarities. We are all in this thing called life together. We need to do it with civility, with love. We need to work harder to get to know each other better, to learn how to understand and love each other as God intended. God will never stop loving people; neither should we.

There are two sides to a coin, two ways (or more) of looking at things. We need to work together to share life's hard journey and help lift each other up instead of tearing each other down. The Lord helps those who help themselves (and others)!

"Those who trust in the Lord will find new strength.

They will soar high on wings like eagles; they will run and not grow weary. They will walk and not faint" (Isa 40:31).

I give thanks to all the people who have entered my life, especially those that have arrived since my better half was called home to Heaven. Over the years, some people have remained, blessing my life with their presence. Some have left, moving on when the purpose for our time together was fulfilled. Both have helped shape me to who I have become.

I leave you with my prayers for you all. All I ask is that you pray for me and I'll pray for you. God Bless!

Bob Reuscher, known to some folks as Pappy, some call him Bob-a-doo. He loves his family that continues to grow with good hearted sons and daughters. He loves being outdoors in mother nature, walking on God's earth, working in the garden, and feeding birds in his backyard. He lives by his "country boy at heart" mantra: "Nature is Natural. It is what God wants us to be, naturally true to His Nature.

God Never Said Life Would Be Easy
By Sue

I love God and I know He loves me. I consider myself a Christ-follower, but as an independent "type-A personality" woman, it is often humanly and spiritually impossible to pray continually, to be thankful in all circumstances, to trust Him completely, and to wait patiently. I have to let it go, get out of my own way, and willingly and fully rely on God.

Following the path God places us on is not always easy but the blessings for being faithful can only be stamped "Made in Heaven by the Master." If I think about me too much, I panic, try to do it on my own, and forget He is walking beside me.

In March 2010, I was in a pit of unbearable pain. I knew I had to crawl out of disbelief, anger, contempt, denial, self-pity, and unworthiness. It took an enormous amount of courage to walk into a Monday night Celebrate Recovery at my church and seek out the Prayer Room. The Prayer Room is an extremely special place on Monday nights. In a private, cozy room, you sit on soft couches with 4 Christian prayer warriors – 3 women and 1 man.

I cannot express what happened that night in that prayer room but it could not have been anything but a miracle. I was shaking and hurting so bad, crying so uncontrollably. I could not see faces clearly, yet I do remember the face of a sister who passed me a box of Kleenex so I would not further embarrass myself. I was facing a heart-breaking decision. I did not know what to do because either way would lead me down an unfamiliar and frightening road.

After I spilled my guts, relaying in detail the unspeakable situation and answering gentle questions asked for clarity, my brother in

Christ, Robert, asked me to close my eyes. His voice was pleasant and soothing. I sat quietly for a moment and felt wrapped in peace. "Tell us where you are, Sue." I felt myself being drawn up and this is what I saw, experienced, and believe happened with all my heart and spirit:

I am flying. I'm a bird flying so high. I feel the wind on my face and the power in my wings. Looking around the world is so beautiful. Something is catching my attention down below. As I drop down closer, I see what it is. It's a pool of calm water surrounded by mountains.

I land on the edge and look up to see a fierce waterfall pouring torrents of water into the pool, but the pool remains quiet and smooth. There is not even a ripple touching the shore. In fact, it is so clear; I can see something at the bottom. It looks like a huge rock. I have no fear. I must see that rock closer.

I dive in. It's not a rock, it's an opening. I am drawn in swiftly, rushing forward. I pop up and am on a beach. A wonderful beach with everything I love the most. In this experience, I am me, not a bird. I love the beach. I sit and feel the warm glorious sun healing my body, caressing my shoulders. I smell the salt water on the breeze that's coming off the crashing waves swirling up close to my feet. I love it, here is my happy place. I sit still just soaking in peace, love, and joy. I don't know how long.

Faintly I heard Robert's voice, "Sue, is anyone with you?"

I feel a presence full of love, before I see with my eyes.

"I'm sitting here with Jesus," I reply.

206

I'm not amazed or excited or blown away, just normal and safe and loved. I sense Jesus loves the beach too.

I am annoyed to be disturbed when Robert asks, "What color are His eyes?"

Jesus turns full face and looks directly at me. "His eyes are so blue. I can see forever."

Robert asked, "Now ask Him the question you came into this room with."

"Jesus, what should I do?" We both stand up, and after walking slightly ahead of me, He turns and says, "Wait, Witness, and Withhold, for Me." Things fade.

I open my eyes, no longer full of tears, and look out to see others in the room with tears streaming down their faces. We are all holding hands. With truth and belief on his face, Robert said, "Sue, you have just been baptized in the Holy Spirit." I see nods of affirmation and looks of amazement from the circle of believers. Two hours after I walked into that room as a wreck, I walked out blessed.

I wanted to dissect every item of that event - flying, the pond, diving in, why the beach, what was Jesus wearing, what did He mean "wait, witness, and withhold?" It was agonizing. I wanted a step-by-step map of how to make a horrible betrayal and infidelity go away.

How was I supposed to deal with my feelings ranging from hate, repulsion, pity, compassion, and maybe just a tiny feeling of doing what He tells me to do in so many ways, like "forgive?" No way! Impossible! What about my self-esteem, my hurt? What would others think of me if I forgave such an unforgiveable travesty? And the humiliation!

Eight years later, I have spiritually grown *because* it was hard. Life is not always easy and light. It is full of trials and tests. Life is not that hard when we rest in Him. I had to trust God to give me His strength and patience, to wait on His timing. I relied on His joy and courage to witness. I had to trust His wisdom to withhold judgment and use His "everlasting" love to forgive.

My marriage not only survived but has grown stronger by living in His Word. At 80, my Lord has placed me in jail ministry. I carry His Word and a seed of hope to incarcerated women in addiction who desire to find recovery through Jesus in the safety of a structured Christ-centered recovery home.

Isaiah 40:31

[31] but they who wait for the LORD shall renew their strength; they shall mount up with wings like eagles; they shall run and not be weary; they shall walk and not faint.

Proverbs 3:5-6
[5] Trust in the LORD with all your heart and lean not on your own understanding;
[6] in all your ways submit to Him, and He will make your paths straight.

1 Thessalonians 5:16-18
[16] Rejoice always, [17] pray continually, [18] give thanks in all circumstances; for this is God's will for you in Christ Jesus.

Matthew 6: 14–15

[14] For if you forgive other people when they sin against you, your heavenly Father will also forgive you. [15] But if you do not forgive others their sins, your Father will not forgive your sins.

Sue is the program director of God Beyond the Bars. Her passion is to carry God's Word and His promise of unconditional love, hope, and forgiveness to women in Roane, Morgan, and Anderson County jails in Tennessee. She resides in Oak Ridge, TN.

Turning the Old Leaf
Scott Smith

I have always been a bit melancholy, for a happy kid. I have always been friendly, for a shy guy. I have always been faithful, for a doubter. There has always been some kind of trouble that has always just been right below the surface, hidden so no one could see or judge.

Not many people have been aware of the trials or tribulations that I have had along this path. My troubles aren't much different than many others I have discovered. Seemingly though, I have been through so many "hard times" that I felt like I was either destined for greatness like Job from the Bible or fated to be doomed like Job from the Bible. That may not make sense to anyone but me. However, when they are your trials, any analogy you want can make total sense.

It seems as though when we go through trials it feels like we are the only ones facing it. That problem and in that moment, the only person's problems that exist are yours. That is when I had a moment with God.

My moments with God have never seemed like much more than a spark of an idea or a burning confirmation of the spirit, but they are entirely unique to my normal. My faith, and to be honest, my doubts, have all been rooted in what appears to be anomalies. I go through my day-to-day life in a state of balance, living a status quo, a kind of "Scottiostasis". It hasn't been easy to see the path or to know the direction that the Lord would have me go. Looking back on it, I have had a bit of a haphazard life.

I am a product of a mid- 90's divorce boom that shaped my life a lot. I lived with both parents having custody at some time or another. There was a constant battle over which parent was going to take care of my sister and I and who had the means to. Visitation

210

time was always a matter of resentment for one parent or the other. There were several times when arguments became physical amongst my parents and my sister and I would try and stop them. Ultimately we ended up hiding in my sister's closet until either the deputies came or we heard car doors slam and my mom's car drive away.

This was life growing up. Sure there were good times and I have some fond memories, but it has left my life tainted by the bad times. I have been through my own divorce, abuse, infidelity, mental illness, addiction, and heartbreak. In the course of my adulthood I have been blessed many times. I have been fortunate to have built good friendships, repaired relationships with some from the past, and the greatest blessing has been having three kids I wouldn't trade for all the riches the world has to offer. Though I count these blessings every day, life has continued to be hard. The hardest thing I've dealt with has been to lose a child.

During my first marriage my oldest son was born. It was a surprise when we got pregnant. We had taken precautions to postpone parenthood. We wanted kids and planned to have a family, but our time table and the will of the Lord can often differ. It happened so fast for us. She got pregnant after 3 months of being married. In spite of our initial plans, we were ecstatic and considered it an adventure. After our son was born, we decided that we wanted to wait a bit longer to have more kids because of our age. We were 20 and 19 and had only been married 13 months when our son was born.

Things were rocky learning how to be a married couple and parents. We were in church and considered ourselves devout Christians. That helped start a good foundation, but we also allowed the secular world to influence us which made things difficult. We hoped that we would be faithful and live righteously, but being young and having past history of habits, it became easy for us to falter.

My wife was diagnosed with mental illness and I too suffered from depression and anxiety. Due to behaviors caused by the ups and downs of disorders, it became very hard for us to be together. Both of us were products of divorced homes and though we tried to do things "right," neither of us felt we were prepared or knew how to be married. So we separated and subsequently divorced, which was the worst possible thing we could have done, but it is ultimately the choice we made.

I remarried after a little while. We were both single parents and decided to build our family together. We were a happy little family of four for a good while. It always felt like a yours and mine relationship with our kids so we decided to go for a "Yours, Mine, and Ours" family. What then seemed like forever happened almost instantaneously. We had our third child together. He was what I thought made our family whole, the missing link. We were doing well, both in college, and working. Our kids were growing and so were we. Then life happened.

Like I said, I suffer from depression and suffer is sometimes an understatement. Shortly after our son was born I was knocked into a tailspin. I lost my job, was struggling in school, and financial ends were becoming harder and harder to meet. I began to plummet and I couldn't knock this feeling of failure. I began to dig myself into a proverbial hole. Lost in my own thoughts, that hole became my own personal prison.

During this time, I started having thoughts of harming myself. It's something that I have dealt with since I was a teen. Depression and anxiety caused me to question a lot of things and the paternity of my Ex-Wife's daughter came into play for some reason. In my head I fixated on thought. My youngest son had just been born, but I was still suspicious if I could have been the father to her daughter who she conceived while we were beginning our separation.

One day, I got the nerve to ask. The answer was devastating. I found out from my first wife that during our separation she had been pregnant with our child. She had an I.U.D. removed during the pregnancy, causing miscarriage. This was a huge blow. I was already not in a good state of mind and this hit like a ton of bricks. When I got the news, it had been years since the miscarriage happened, but it didn't make it any easier to take the news. I would hold on to the pain and grief for several more years.

This past year, I began a 12-step program to help overcome some of my history, my depression, and anxiety. I was going to turn over a new leaf. I was doing well and making progress. I finally began to pray like I should, acting in faith and not just searching for logic. I was doing the work to get to recovery.

I had to address my past and something about losing a baby kept coming up. I couldn't figure out why this was so paramount in my mind. I had thought that even though it hurt, I had buried the pain deep. The pain was still there. I had never really talked about it. I thought I confronted and embraced the idea of this missing child. I had allowed a statuette of a little angel become a representation of that child I never mourned. But why was it still bothering me so much now? I thought that I was handling it. I had never brought it up again with my ex-wife and we never discussed what all had happened or how she dealt with it.

As part of my program I decided to try and forgive the past, getting rid of resentments. I came to realize that I had so much hurt and pain associated with this miscarriage, from her not telling me, for not letting me be part of the process. I had to figure out a way to face this. She had suffered through this process too. Feeling that my resentment was possibly deserved, but not fair, I would have to rely on something greater than my own understanding. I finally made a decision. If I was going to turn over a new leaf, I had to find this old leaf and turn it over first.

If I was going to become stronger, now was the time to put my faith in God and ask him for healing. I was in the midst of a second divorce and beginning to waver in my diligence of prayer again. I was going through so much again. I felt like I was on rewind and searching for the same lessons to learn.

I finally got up the nerve to confront and work out all these issues with my ex-wife. I didn't want to be driven back into a depressive state and not be able to come back. I put it all out there to God. After much thought, conversation, and deep prayer, I felt prompted to associate a name with this lost child of mine. If I was going to be better, and get better, I had to move. I had to listen. I had to give meaning and purpose to my pain.

I had to turn that old leaf over one final time and accept God in all things. He had a purpose for the child and for the circumstances and loss. I had to get closer to this child, not hide her away in my heart and mind. I had to have a way to connect with her. I had to do something to have a relationship with her spirit. I had to connect a name to her. I named her Autumn.

Scott Smith is an aspiring nature and portrait photographer and technologist who resides in the mountains of East Tennessee. His desire is to capture and create images that change and inspire people's perspective from within. As photography and technology continue to converge, his hope is to use them both for positive changes in this ever changing world. He is a self-proclaimed "Research Librarian for the Lord" with a desire to help others seek and understand the Lord. Through his works, he hopes to reflect the beauty the Lord created in Mankind and Nature.

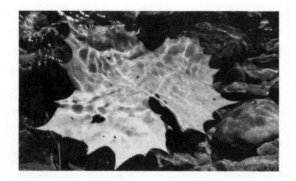

Connecting the Dots
by Tom Sudman

Fully Relying on God (FROG) to me is not an event. It is a process. I call this process "How God connects the dots in my life." The first part of this process for me, and for many, was the most difficult. It was coming to the realization that in the big picture of life I am but a dot. If counting only people, there are 7.7 Billion other dots in this world with me. If counting stars, there are over 400 Billion stars in our galaxy. There are 170 Billion Galaxies in the Universe.

When viewing the universe and its magnitude of numbers, I view my share of time and space in this design as a dot. Without God connecting me to other dots, life can lead rapidly to a feeling of insignificance.

A clue to connectivity in God's design for us is the fact that the human body is made up of 37 trillion cells, some of which are holding other cells in place. One of these cells that hold other cells together is a Laminin Cell, which is in the shape of a cross. "He is before all things, and in him all things hold together" (Colossians 1:17 NIV). Thus, our soul and self are housed in another huge numbers game, much like the universe itself. Thank God that He is in charge of these huge design concepts and this is not a random creation.

During your education you may start to visualize yourself being connected to other dots. The dots that you have been connected to like family, friends, and school have formed "circles of dots." You have become part of these communities, but dots begin to exit these circles because of death, moves, and changes like graduating from school. New circles are also forming around work, church, hobbies, and neighbors. You now have a circle called family with different dots than the original circle you called family (Genesis 2:2). In this family circle, there is a dot called spouse with circles of dots. They may be the same or different than your former circles. Circles of dots that once seemed static become increasingly more fluid and more numerous.

Now in my senior years, I look back on my life and have lots to be thankful for. Even though I am but a mere dot, the other dots that have been included in my life have made great things happen. The results of my life are clearly seen in the dots that I have been connected to: my wife, my children, my friends, and people that I have met from accomplishing work milestones. All of the circles have not been positive. Some dots within some of the circles were not constructive, but in all cases, my life is better defined when I was part of a circle, not when I was by myself as the dot.

So how did I get connected to my dots? The connective stories are so numerous that they would be a book itself. I can tell you that all of them point to God because there is no other explanation for people being where they were, when they were. Connecting dots was not an act on my part, but through God putting people in my life. Randomness would have produced a different result than if a person simply provided what I needed, when I needed it. There was, and is, divine design. I needed to still invite dots into the circle, but He clearly placed them where they could be invited. In addition, I have clearly seen Him place me in other people's life with no other possible explanation.

My favorite bible verse that explains why connecting dot works is from Matthew 18:20: "For where two or three gathers in my name, there am I with them." When you understand God is responsible for the circle, you are building in His name. When you invite Him into your life, then you get the results you would expect with God as part of your team. So, when you bring about two dots, you really get three. That third dot, not your ego, makes a circle and it's no longer a dot. That super circle and His presence allow it to interact with purpose to survive in something as huge as the universe with its numbers as described above.

God dispatched the apostles in Luke 10:1: "after this the Lord appointed 72 others and sent them two by two." In Mark 6:7: "Calling the twelve to him, he began to send them out two by two." Both these situations were limited human resource events, yet He halved the number of groups to connect dots that maintained power by gathering two or more in one place. Growing a dot does not produce the same results as connecting two dots in His name.

In the end, I have been but a dot, but the power of my existence is from other dots and circles in which He has allowed me to exist because of His presence in those circles. I believe the eternal world will follow this design: a circle has no beginning or end. Jesus calls us to be part of one body in which He is the head (think, main dot). We get to meet God and have eternal life with the ultimate **circle** of dots. "Thy kingdom come, Thy will done; on earth as it is in heaven."

In a circle with Jesus, the cells of my body may be finite and go to dust, but my soul is still a dot in an eternal circle relationship with Him. "But whoever is united with the Lord is one with him in spirit" (1Cor. 6:17). We are but a dot, but God connects the dots in our life and always will. We were not predestined to be a mere dot, but a purpose driven, loved and connected dot.

Mother Teresa speaks to this when she said: "If we have no peace, it is because we have forgotten that we belong to each other." An unconnected dot dies, or otherwise, becomes insignificant. The dot that chooses to become part of Jesus' circle (the body of Christ) lives on forever and operates within the significant and all-wise will of God. Somehow this all makes sense to me. I hope it does to you.

Tom Sudman is an entrepreneur who has founded several businesses including Digital AV (www.digitalav.com) which is in its 36th year. In retirement he spends his time in the Sudman Foundation (www.sudmanfoundation.org). He and his family are blessed to live in God's creation of the mountains of East Tennessee.

Fully Relying on Drugs
By Theodule Smith*

"to bind up the brokenhearted, to proclaim liberty to the captives, and the opening of the prison to them that are bound" -- taken from Isaiah 61:1, later quoted by Jesus Christ, as reported in Luke 4:16-18 (KJV, Public Domain)

"Joseph died," said Alan. I had met Joseph at an addiction treatment center. Shortly afterward, he relapsed and died of an overdose.

"Elliot died," Matt's message stated. I had met Elliott during a drug court jail visit when he was about to be released. A few months later he relapsed and died of an overdose.

"Alicia died," Gavin told me. I had met Alicia at a local church. She had been living in a recovery halfway house and attending 12-step meetings and church services. The last time I saw her, at a discount store, she was being escorted by a store security officer to the room where they hold shoplifting suspects until the police come to place them under arrest and take them to jail. She was then evicted from the house and had returned to her home town, where she died within days. I do not know what went wrong.

This list could go on. The author of this article is a recovering chemical addict, and I would like to offer a few suggestions for those struggling with chemical addiction or other enslaving vices.

These are not the steps used by most recovery fellowships and treatment centers. They are guidelines gleaned from my own struggle to overcome addiction and from several years of experience in long term recovery, as well as from observations of the successes and failures of others.

1. Seek medical evaluation and treatment. This is especially important if you have other medical or mental health problems in addition to your primary addiction. If you do not have insurance or resources, keep on politely asking and seeking help. You may become discouraged. Keep trying anyway.

2. Try to avoid the people, places, and activities that would tempt you to "use", whether that means alcohol, street drugs, prescription pills, gambling, pornography, promiscuity, overeating, etc. For some of us this may mean an abrupt and drastic change of residence or employment. If you cannot avoid dangerous circumstances, consider minimizing your risk by taking a safe trusted person with you. Keep your guard up.

3. Begin replacing the dangerous people, places, and activities with better and safer ones. Recognize that some of your attempts may not be successful, and that some of the "new" people might judge you or try to use you. Avoid them and keep trying anyway.

4. Keep reminding yourself that it is not okay to use, and try to avoid allowing your mind to dwell on thoughts of using. This is critical.

5. Avoid holding on to your "stuff". This does not just mean whatever possessions you might have. It means the stuff that is inside you: your thoughts, feelings, beliefs, values, attitudes, and experiences. It means your worldview and your belief system -- the way you feel about yourself and the way you perceive and respond to people and events around you. Be willing to patiently evaluate --

and to begin to revise -- all these things. Expect this to take months ... and years.

6. Do not too quickly discard your "stuff" or adopt anyone else's "stuff" or belief system. You will find that others, whether at treatment centers, 12-step meetings, or churches, will insist that they have found the way. Do not be too quick to believe them. Be willing to patiently listen, observe, read, reflect, evaluate, pray, learn.

7. Recognize that setting your life in order might take a long time, and that some things might never be mended or restored. Your life in recovery will not be perfect; no one's life is. You might have to stay at a shelter. You might have to go to jail for things you did in active addiction. You might have to live with some of the consequences of your mistakes and failures. Do not be discouraged. Keep trying to do the right thing anyway.

8. Keep seeking a right and better relationship with The Creator. I do not recommend creating your own Creator. You might wonder why this one is last. That does not mean that it is of lesser importance. These are not steps to be worked in a prioritized order; they are suggestions and guidelines for today and for the long term. Please reread them and note that each one reflects the concept of endurance.

Best wishes.

* All the names in this article, including that of the author, have been changed.

Theodule Smith is the pen name of a recovering chemical addict living near Knoxville, Tennessee. He teaches music. This is his first article. If you would like to contact him, please email TheoduleSmith314@gmail.com

Cycling Back to God
By Tony Twilla

It was a beautiful sunlit morning on July 6, 2002. My then son-in-law and I could think of nothing more fun than to go mountain bike riding at Norris Dam State Park. So we took off, ready for a rejuvenating and relaxing day. We knew that Norris Dam would be a safe place to ride. Neither of us were "rough and tumble" riders. We just loved being outdoors and pedaling those bikes.

We had pedaled hard up a long, steep gravel road, enjoying every minute of the ride and beauty around us. We reached the top and knew it would be an exhilarating ride going down the hill to the bottom. Neither of us was trying to race or show off. We used our brakes and were careful riding on the gravel.

I was about halfway down the hill, enjoying the ride, when my bike slid over into a ditch. I went over the handlebars landing headfirst. I was immediately paralyzed and lay in the ditch in a fetal position unable to move any part of my body. My son-in-law was biking ahead of me and had already gone down the hill. When he realized that I had not reached the bottom behind him, he went back looking for me, finding me in the ditch. He immediately called 911 and an ambulance arrived shortly thereafter.

At this point, it's important to note that I was not afraid nor was I in pain. I knew immediately that God was going to use this situation to draw me back to Him. You see, for some time I had been doing all the things that are expected of Christians; yes, even praying, but it was a mere attempt to maintain a spiritual façade and satisfy what I thought His requirements were. For many months before this accident, my heart had been far from God and I knew it, but I had done nothing to rekindle our relationship. I had full assurance that while God did not cause this accident, He was going to use it to draw me back to Him.

224

Now, back to the particulars of my story. I was immediately taken to the University of Tennessee Hospital where I was examined by a neurosurgeon. My spinal cord at the C3/4 level had been severely bruised. I had no movement from my chest down. For someone who had always been independent and doing everything without assistance, not wanting or accepting help from others, this was a severe blow.

After a week at UT Hospital, I was transferred to Patricia Neal Rehabilitation Center in Knoxville. My wife, daughter, and son-in-law took turns staying with me since I could do nothing on my own. If my nose needed blowing, someone had to hold a tissue for me. Someone had to feed me every meal. I could move my head and see but that was about all. The doctors said it was not likely that I would ever walk or resume any semblance of a normal life. But, even with this prognosis, I knew God was working it to draw me back to Him.

I asked my daughter to put Scriptures in large print on the wall across from my bed so I could see them. Frankly, I don't remember praying much, I just knew that God was busy reconciling me to Himself. My daughter sent emails to friends across the country asking them to pray for God's healing.

One day after being at Patricia Neal for about four weeks, I looked down and to my amazement I could wiggle a big toe. Wow, what a huge thing for someone who could move nothing! Gradually as days went by and I received physical therapy, movement started traveling up my legs very slowly. I was a determined man, knowing that I must do all I could do and leave the rest to God. It surely was not an easy task.

Every time the staff would stand me up, my blood pressure would go so low that they had to lay me down again. Eventually I could stand, but not walk. I learned to walk by being put in a harness suspended from a frame and looking down to see where to place my feet as I tried to walk.

After eight weeks at Patricia Neal I was sent home in an electric wheelchair without assurance that I would ever truly walk again. Well, I ditched the wheelchair soon after being released, graduated to a walker, and then to no aides at all. Movement returned to my arms and hands but certainly not with the mobility I had prior to the accident. My right side to this day has very little feeling and is weak. My left side is a bit stronger with slightly more sensation.

So, I've told you all about the physical improvement. Today I walk, haltingly, but I walk. I do pretty much all the things I did before, but much more slowly. I have learned some ingenious ways of making things work when I don't have full physical ability.

By far the greatest miracle is my relationship with God has grown so sweet and deep, sometimes indescribable. A heart that had grown cold is now on fire to live a life that brings Him glory. Prayer has become an ongoing conversation with my Father. Don't misunderstand, there are still plenty of holes and cracks in me that need repair by His grace (just ask my wife and daughter). I still seek to deepen my walk with Him each day (many times throughout the day).

So, dear ones, that's my story and I'm sticking to it. I would not change one thing. If not having the accident meant that my heart would have remained cold towards my Savior, I would opt for lying in that ditch and dealing with the consequences of a spinal cord injury. Whatever struggles you may be facing today, allow God to use them to shape you into what you could never be without those struggles.

Tony Twilla is a retired human resources manager. He has taught men's Bible studies for many years and is actively involved in prison ministry teaching. He and his wife of 55 years have two adult children and three grandchildren.

A Faith Life Unfolding
By Jane Walker

1978 joyous wedding bells peal.
God reveals my soul mate now.
1981 first child's birth squeal.
What a miracle. Wait. God, show me how.

1982 a second child here so soon you say?
God, walk me through post-partem depression.
1983 Third child on the way?
Wait? What? Regression is the impression.

1984 Third sweet child makes her dainty start.
Diapers, potty training, Mr. Rogers, library story hour.
Three kids under four, no family in town – not for the faint of
heart.
Hardly time for a spare breath or even a soaking shower.

1985 Financially committed: our kids are going to Christian
schools.
Relying on God by force of habit and sheer hope.
One income and no extra money. We must be fools.
Growing in familial love, we joyously, but tenuously, cope.

1990 Husband changes his employment.
A little scary: new town, public schools, new church.
Family takes up camping and cycling for enjoyment.
Hunkering down, drawing near. Fully relying on God again in this
lurch.

1992 Mom back to work after a graced ten-year child-care stint.
Sunbeam lands on a help-wanted bulletin in the church pew.
(Yes, to hear God's call, I guess I needed that obvious glint.)
Joy. Teaching French and Religion in a faith-based venue.

Who's cooking dinner? Kids cleaning their bathrooms.
What an adjustment for our little clan!
Just hanging on. Life is ripping by zoom-zoom.
Is this frantic feeling a part of God's plan?

1996 Husband's next job change feels like a move up, at last.
New town. New church. Schools focused on God's way.
Dream home, science fairs, and home improvement tasks.
Take a breath. Faith, family, and work build in a balanced ballet.

1997 My soul mate is diagnosed with advanced colon cancer.
Five months later, forty years old, he has slipped past the pain and
into God's hands.
Didn't see this coming; Didn't have an answer.
The earthly cornerstone of our family unit gone. Can my heart
stand?

No time for self-pity. Get up and be there for these 'tween and teen
children of mine.
At last I clearly understand why God sent three children in four
years.
They needed every marvelous minute of that dear Dad time.
Finally I could see and trust his plan. God was wiping away my
fears.

Folks at my school became my extended family so caring.
God's love exemplified, magnified, and freely given by those kind
souls.
My children and I encountered love daring.
Our angels on Earth and our saints in Heaven encasing us in their
folds.

Through the years the heart heals under such gentle care.
Life refuses to slow down.
1999 First child graduates high school ready to take to the air.
Off to her dad's alma mater – college bound.

2000 My middle child has motorcycle accident on his
Confirmation night.
Bed-ridden and in and out of surgery for a year.
Another treacherously close encounter with death's fright.
The Holy Spirit standing strong. Sending strength to fight fear.

Eighteen times through eighteen surgeries, with God I talked.
Silly woman. God was there well beyond those eighteen times!
His voice ever-present as we built strength and again walked.
Throughout that year more angels and saints appeared as signs.

2002 Third child, the baby, goes off to college seven hours away.
Wait! How can I be an empty-nester?
Torrents of tears on a long drive home on a rainy day.
Where is my husband, God? The deal was to do this together.

2003 Living alone. Giving my children room to explore.
Privileged to be immersed in a faith environment, my work is my
rock.
Each day I am conduit to touch lives and, by example, perhaps
open faith's door.
This is beautiful, vocational work - giving back to teens who
knock.

2006 Job responsibilities increase.
Too busy to faithfully maintain the proper relationship.
All out of balance. No inner peace.
Humbling. Relearning to put God in charge of this trip.

2013 Grandchildren begin arriving and deepen life's wonders.
Sacrificial love exponentially expounds.
God at every hobbling step enlightening my human blunders.
A deeper faith resonates. Learning to listen for God's sounds.

Today? I plunge into an ever-intoxicating dive;
Exploring the mysteries of a faith life unfolding.
Learning to put God above all strife.
In Christ further molding.

Jane Walker serves as Academic Dean at a faith-based high school in Knoxville, TN. She is continually nourished in her parenting and grandparenting roles. As in introvert, she enjoys outside activities including camping, kayaking, and home improvement projects.

Everything's Fine
By Michael Wayne Smith

I started writing songs in the early-to-mid 90s until 2000. Life got busy, priorities changed and the songs stopped coming. In 2001, my family and I started attending a church near Knoxville, TN. I initially just wanted to blend in and was happy with people not knowing I had any musical talent, but within a few weeks word got out that I sang.

The next thing I knew I was singing in their choir. Other choir members heard my singing voice and approached the worship leader to say that I should be considered for their praise team. Just like that I spent the next 7 years on the church's praise team.

In spring of 2006, I began to feel that God wanted more from me, musically and ministerially. Although I enjoyed singing and worshiping on the praise team, I felt God's plan for me was shifting in a different direction.

On a Tuesday evening, I prayed God would give me a sign of what He wanted for my life. Above all, I wanted to be in His will. That Friday, I wrote a song titled "Calvary Stands in My Way." At the time, I didn't think much of it. I was glad to have written a new song, especially since it had been 6 years since doing so.

The very next day, I wrote another song titled "Welcome Home." It was then when it dawned on me that God was giving me the sign I had asked for. Finally, on Sunday, I wrote a song that eliminated any doubt what God was telling me. I knew that through this song God was calling me to step out and share my gift to a larger audience.

That song was "Everything's Fine." I took the title from a phrase people hear every day in the work place, at home, church, etc. We casually ask people how they are doing and they say "everything's fine" because inside they are too afraid to say how things really are. Thankfully, through Jesus Christ, we can say with confidence and faith that everything will be fine because we know God will never leave nor forsake us.

I had never written a song like that and although it was relatively simple, it spoke volumes. The first line is "I just heard the news this morning." Who doesn't get bad news from time to time? The song captured listeners from the start.

Everything's Fine was the confirmation I asked God for. Although I knew I would be stepping down from the church praise team, I remained another 2 years while I continued writing songs and eventually recording a CD.

By October of 2008, the new CD was finished. A year later, "Everything's Fine" was released as my first radio single. Within weeks, the song started getting major airplay. Then, came the phone calls, emails, and letters. If it wasn't someone contacting me to share their story of how this song helped them in some way, it was a church asking me if I could come and sing for them.

It seemed that my whole ministry was built overnight all because of one song, but I know this was always God's plan for me. I have been sharing *Everything's Fine* for the last 10 years and always count it an honor to stand on a stage and sing that song. It is still my most requested song. I shudder to think if I had not walked this path God laid out for me how different things would be.

EVERYTHING'S FINE

<u>Verse One</u>
I JUST HEARD THE NEWS THIS MORNING

I CAN'T IMAGINE HOW YOU FEEL

I WISH I KNEW THE WORDS TO SAY

TO MAKE IT NOT SEEM SO REAL

Chorus
BUT EVERYTHING'S FINE, EVERYTHING'S OK.

I JUST HAD A TALK WITH JESUS AND HE SAID

HELP IS ON THE WAY.

SO JUST HANG ON AND DON'T LOSE SIGHT.

SOON THE WAITING WILL BE OVER

AND HE WILL MAKE YOUR BURDEN LIGHT,

EVERYTHING'S FINE.

Verse Two
NOW YOU MAY THINK YOU'VE LOST YOUR WAY.

YOUR WORLD IS SPINNING ROUND AND ROUND.

BUT WHAT A FRIEND YOU HAVE IN JESUS.

HE WILL NEVER LET YOU DOWN.

Bridge
WELL, I KNOW THINGS SEEM SO HARD

BUT KEEP THE FAITH AND DON'T LOSE HEART.

Written By Michael Wayne Smith
4/3/2006
*Copyright © 2006 Fifth Sunday Publishing (BMI), All Rights
Reserved.*

*Michael and his wife Kelley have been married for 26 years and
reside in Oak Ridge, TN. They have 2 daughters, Kerri and Kasey.
Michael is a full time gospel recording artist and travels, with
Kelley, across the country sharing God's love and encouragement
through his original music.*

*Since starting their ministry in 2009, Michael has released 7 studio
albums, a "live" concert DVD, and has had many charting songs.
But, most importantly, they are doing their part in building God's
Kingdom and seeing many people encouraged through his music.*

*For more information regarding the music of Michael Wayne
Smith please visit his website at www.michaelwaynesmith.com.*

CPSIA information can be obtained
at www.ICGtesting.com
Printed in the USA
LVHW021008081019
633523LV00016B/1614/P

9 781946 419064